A STORY TO TELL:

THE DIACONATE

Morag Crawford DCS

Morag Crawford DCS

125 years of Diaconal ministry in Scotland

December 2013

British Library Cataloguing in Publication Data:
A Catalogue record for this publication
is available from the British Library.

ISBN: 978-0-9927814-0-8

Published by The Diaconate Council of the Church of Scotland
c/o The Church Offices, 121 George Street, Edinburgh EH2 4YN

Printed by
Winter and Simpson Print, 16 Dunsinane Avenue, Dundee
DD2 3QT

Table Of Contents

The history of the Diaconate in the Church of Scotland is quite complex – much has happened in 125 years. Telling our story involves looking at how separate strands of work came to be mingled; at how the policy-makers of the Church thought of Diaconal work and of women's work as time went on. This part of our story has its own importance; yet by itself it fails to show the human aspects: the stories of lives of service, dedicated to Christ.

Chapters 4, 8, 11 and 12, marked above with an *, are therefore dedicated to short biographical sketches. The placing of these chapters in the book is appropriate to the stage the overall story has reached; and within each of these chapters, the stories are told in chronological order and are chosen with a view to demonstrating the breadth of work and vision, as well as for their own interest. Where possible the individuals concerned have been consulted and thanks are due to them for their willing consent to what is said and for their cooperation with the research.

List of Illustrations

Thanks are due to the Hanney family of Cardoness, the descendants of Alice Maxwell, who gave permission to reprint pictures contained in the book by Miss Maxwell's sister, Mrs Horatio Macrae, *Alice Maxwell Deaconess* (1920). These are marked * in the following list. All other pictures are those of the author or from the Diaconate Archive at the Church Offices.

Acknowledgements

Thanks are due to the many people who have encouraged, helped and supported me in collating this book much of which has been researched from Assembly Reports, Diaconal Newsletters and archives. Thanks to those who contributed personal stories and pictures.

Thanks too to the Hanney family of Cardoness, the descendants of Alice Maxwell, who gave permission to use the pictures of her in the book written by her sister Mrs Horatio Macrae.

A special thanks is due to Frank Bardgett for the countless hours spent editing the work and giving advice.

Morag Crawford
November 2013

Foreword

A Deacon: what is a Deacon? What do they do? Are there many of you? Is that the same as a Deacons' Court? These are just some of the questions Deacons get asked. This book will answer some of these questions and it will tell you so much more.

The ministry of the Diaconate in the Church of Scotland is now 125 years old, but our history has never been recorded in one single volume. There are individual biographies, lectures and so on but it was difficult for anyone to get a clear picture.

Putting this history into one story was long overdue: the story is worth telling and it deserves to be heard and known. The journey of the Deaconesses in the Church of Scotland began with the December 1988 'Setting Apart' of Lady Grisell Baillie, as the Rev. Professor Charteris sought to fulfil his vision for the gifts of the women of the Church being integral to the mission of the Church. 'A Story to Tell' combines the story of the Deaconesses who followed in the steps of Lady Grisell Baillie with accounts of the origins and work of the Parish Sisters, the Deaconess Nurses and the Church Sisters who over time arose within the Established, Free and the United Free Churches of Scotland.

We, as the present Diaconate of the Church of Scotland, are grateful to Morag Crawford MSc, DCS for researching, writing, collating the information, and bringing out the stories of these almost unheard of women, and now of course men, who have worked at the frontline, the margins of society and across the world over all these years: women and men called by God to a Diaconal vocation of lifelong service to God and his Church.

Jane M. Martin
Secretary to the Diaconate
Council of the Church of
Scotland

1

My Journey

*'This is my command: be resolute; do not be fearful or dismayed for
the Lord your God is with you wherever you go.'*
(Joshua 1: 9, New English Bible)

These are the words written in a Bible presented to me by my home
congregation of Bathgate High Church on my appointment as a
Deaconess; they have proved to be a great encouragement over the
years particularly at times when things have been difficult.

In a little book on my bookshelf entitled 'Baby's Days' an entry
reads: *'Went to Sunday School 18 September 1949 age 2 years 3
months'*. And so began my faith journey. I'm told in the afternoon I
lined up my dolls, tried to teach them 'Jesus loves me' and told them
a Bible story. This began a pattern that followed through childhood:
Church often twice on a Sunday; Sunday School; playing at Sunday
Schools with the dolls or with my cousins when we visited my
grandfather's. At three I was inspired by the story, read to me from
the back page of the *Girl* comic, of Mary Slessor of Calabar. That
was what I would do when I grew up – go to Africa as a teacher.
When we played at school, I was always the teacher. At ten my
mother died; I still wanted to be a teacher but could I leave my father
on his own to do missionary work? At 15, a few weeks before the
end of term, I suddenly decided I was leaving school. When my
former Primary Leader and Girls' Brigade Captain heard she tutted
and said *'A good teacher going to waste!'* I went to work in Bathgate
telephone exchange, going through the various stages until I reached
acting supervisor level, involved with training. I didn't forget the
comment from the Brigade Captain – the niggle was still there – to
teach.

I taught in the Beginners' and Primary Sunday Schools from the age
of twelve going on to be Beginners' and Primary Leader, organising

weekly Sunday School Teacher training classes. I attended training myself through Sunday School teachers' weekends, and a correspondence course run by the Scottish Sunday School Union, coming into contact with Deaconesses who ran these courses, although I did not realise at the time they were Deaconesses. I was also involved as a Girls' Brigade officer and a member of the Congregational Board. One day I drove a Missionary friend to a youth fellowship meeting she was speaking at and there met a Deaconess, Grace Clark (Morrison). My friend encouraged the young folk to think about Overseas Mission and Grace encouraged them to think about home mission work. Was this something I could consider? On making enquiries I received information about the various employing Committees one could apply to at that time but you had to be 21 and have two Highers. I didn't qualify on either count. Night school was an option but life was busy. Seeing an advert for correspondence courses, I started to study this way. Before I sat my exams I wrote to the Deaconess Board again to discover the qualifying age had gone down to 18 and that application for employment was via the Home Board. I applied, was interviewed and was immediately accepted because I was by then a 'mature student' and, having attended Bathgate Academy, I was considered to have the necessary ability for study. I had ten months to wait before starting college. (I later did pass my exams.)

My two years at St Colm's were a wonderful experience. I appreciated the community living, the teaching, the late night discussions, the worship and devotional life, Quiet Days and meeting folks from many different countries. My first student placement was Holy Trinity, Wester Hailes, Edinburgh where I was given an assignment to look at Christian Education. Going into schools I discovered teachers did not really appreciate the Church coming into the school as 'ministers weren't trained to talk to children'. My second placement was at Currie. I was warned it would be a challenging placement as the minister was a radical thinker, I loved my time there. When it came to options for my third year specialised study, because of my interest in education and my experience at Wester Hailes, I wanted to do something on teaching methods. Moyra McCallum DCS and Nancy Allison, tutors at St Colm's, both supported me and I was able to get into the Primary Graduates Course at Moray House. It was to be part-time and I was to work part-time in the Currie congregation, who were also to help finance my third year. As it turned out it was full time at Moray House *and* part-time at Currie.

As I wasn't doing the exams, for essays I was encouraged to explore developments on School and Community and to think about how community and church related to each other. When I went into schools on teaching practice I wondered if this would be the testing point for me – should I have gone into teaching? No, I found I was happy to be there as a Deaconess. My experience stood me in good stead for being accepted in schools when working in parishes.

I was appointed as a probationer Deaconess – my contract saying 'Deaconess' – to Drylaw, Edinburgh and was commissioned on 23 September 1977. There were only a handful of children in Sunday School in a congregation which had once boasted having the biggest Sunday School in Scotland. It wasn't long before I realised we should be doing something else with children: so began mid–week clubs and Holiday clubs run three times a year taking the children on a day trip in the summer. Available material tended to be geared to middle class areas and so with the knowledge gained at Moray House I produced my own material and worksheets.

Work at Drylaw changed as needs changed, ranging from Mothers and Toddlers to unchurched youth, taking them away for weekends, sleeping on the floor in a church hall in the Angus West area, my Presbyterial Council link. They challenged my faith, and my patience! Going home after a particularly difficult evening, I picked up my Bible, opened it at random and the words from 1 Corinthians 13 '*Love never gives up*' jumped out at me: I knew that if I was to show the love of God I couldn't give up on these youngsters. We had many in-depth conversations over games of table tennis, pool, or cards, which they taught me. If there was trouble at the club, they would leave one by one, and going home after I tidied up I would find them all sitting at the foot of my stairs, ready to come in, make coffee and raid the tins for home baking. Once, because they were bored and being a nuisance outside the building, I got them to paint the church kitchen and hall – afterwards they declared '*that was the best week of the school holidays*'. As a reward they asked if they could pitch their tent on my back green – anything to keep them away from the drug scene. (You can't do any of these things nowadays because of child protection and health and safety laws.)

Pastoral care, organising holidays to Craigengower, and setting up a Day Care scheme were all part of the work; the last, being one of the first projects to get Social Work funding for the building, requiring a contract between the Church Extension Committee and Edinburgh Council. Education for children and adults was carried out imaginatively ('learning by stealth' was the expression used at that time) encouraging others to use their gifts and talents. Flower festivals, worship using floral art to depict the church's year, a three year project round building a Palestinian house in the church hall to tell stories of Jesus' life in Palestine – all were part of the creative work involving school, church and community my colleague Ian Gilmour and I as the ministry team enabled folk to undertake.

The supervision and training experience from my 'exchange days' was put to good use in supervising and training students particularly at a time when the Church did not train its supervisors. Over the years I have had students from the Presbyterian Church in Ireland, Church of Scotland, Mauritius, independent students, a Deaconess from the Methodist church, Readers in training as well as ministry. Currently I am a local assessor for those going through the enquiry process for ministry. For a time I tutored for the Training in Learning and Service courses from St Colm's and later the Scottish Churches Open College.[i]

The Diaconate's admittance to the courts of the Church has involved me in Committees at Presbytery and Assembly level; I have served as Moderator of Presbytery and been Interim Moderator of vacant congregations on two occasions.

After twenty-one and a half years at Drylaw I was moved to Rosyth Parish Church where work included Pastoral work, School and

Workplace Chaplaincy, holiday clubs and a project to develop the Church Building. An early project was the initiation of the Rosyth Garden City Association; we now hold annual exhibitions involving the four primary schools and the wider community, attracting over 2,000 visitors in a week. In all my ministry a lot of time has been spent raising money for various projects.

During my time at Drylaw I had been asked to allow my name to go forward as President of Diaconate Council. At the funeral service of Dorothy Gardner DCS, as I listened to the Rev. Mary Levison give the tribute, I thought *'Lord, I can't do this I am not like either of them; I have nothing to give'*. Next thing I received a letter saying I was unanimously elected as President. Maybe I could just do a 'holding job'. God had other plans!! At my first world conference in Nova Scotia, Scotland was asked to host the European Conference in 1994. The group I chaired as President had to find a venue, fund-raise, plan the Conference, involve Guilds and other groups within the Church and community, thus raising the profile of the Diaconate in many different ways. It was a successful and happy conference but it was also a time when the Diaconate was faced with the challenge of the employing committee stopping recruitment.

The end of my time as President of the Council coincided with the end of Rev. David Donaldson's time as Convener of the Diaconate Committee. Sitting in the Church Offices one Monday along with the Secretary, Yvonne Teague, we were considering names for a new Convener. I described the kind of person I thought we should look for, who would take us through the next difficult period. David said, *'I think it should be you Morag'*. I immediately said no and repeated again the qualities we were looking for. David was adamant. I was going to the Methodist Convocation at Swanwick so promised I would consider it and give my answer at the Committee meeting on my return. The weather was bad, I had long waits at stations on my journey, I filled the time by making lists of 'why' and 'why not' I should be Convener. The story of Moses and his excuses comes to mind. To my horror the list of 'whys' grew longer than the 'why nots'. Sharing my story with the Warden and key people in the Methodist Diaconate I thought they would agree with me that we needed someone of standing. Instead they thought it was time for a

Deaconess. The theme of the Bible Studies was from selected verses from Isaiah 41-43 on 'Staying in the hard place'. Not what I wanted to hear! On consulting Kay Ramsay DCS on my return she listened, as Kay did, and asked what I had done about it. I told her and her response was '*You have your answer*'. I became the first and only Deaconess to be Convener of the Diaconate Committee.

It was not an easy time. What were we to do about recruitment and training? I needed to equip myself to look at the issues and found a course at Moray House. Speaking with John Landon, Head of the Department, I found myself on a degree course on Professional Development in spite of the fact I did not have a first degree. My St Colm's training was recognised as such. Receiving great encouragement from all my tutors, the course proved to be a life saver for me as many of the scenarios we looked at on training, management and the place of women in secular society were similar to what I was experiencing within the Committees of the Church. We looked at women in teaching, nursing and social work, and considered whether these were professions or semi professions; and whether their status was because they had been mainly women's roles. We considered identity, and failure to recognise identity by calling people by another name or job title – it was all the Diaconate story. This was what I was reading about in my research of the church archives on the Diaconate and was seeing played out in the Committees. John Landon kept saying to me there was a story to tell and a book to be written.

There is a story to tell of the Diaconate in the Church of Scotland: a story of vision, a story of service, yes and of struggle but stories of remarkable service given by incredible people. What follows in this book in this our 125 anniversary year is that 'Story to Tell'.

2

A Man of Vision

'I commend to you Phoebe a fellow Christian who holds office in the congregation at Cenchreae.' (Romans 16:1)

'....everything must be done – if the old ship is to hold together ten years longer.'

So wrote Rev. Prof. Archibald Charteris to an old friend in 1861. The ship he was referring to was the established Church of Scotland. The years to the end of the century were to see Charteris introduce the Church to visionary ideas for mission from which came the Young Men's Guild, the *Life and Work* magazine and the Woman's Guild. Charteris also wanted to see an organisation for trained women workers in the church. To meet the needs of the time, he proposed the revival in Scotland of the ancient office of Deaconess.

It was into a challenging world that the introduction of the Diaconate to the Church of Scotland took place. The aftermath of the Napoleonic wars and the rapid industrial revolution had seen great changes. The nineteenth century brought the liberation of slaves and the Factories Acts. The industrial revolution meant large populations grew round the new factories and mines, bringing vast movements of population from the country to the cities. By the end of the century towns had grown to a size that could never have been imagined in the eighteenth century. There was a race for riches on the one hand and on the other the products of the industrial revolution brought slums, hunger, poverty, broken lives, ignorance of religion and morals. In the Churches it revived a spirit of missionary enterprise. There was a new fervour in all branches of the Church and in particular the need for mission amongst those moving to the towns. Meanwhile the role of women in society was changing. Although women still were unable to vote, the idea that they should be regarded as *'non persons' in the public world*[ii] waned as society moved from a home-centred economy to an industrial base. As women's work began to develop in British society, so too it did in the church: Elizabeth Fry began to reform prisons in the first decades of the 19th century, while the first women missionaries had gone out from Scotland in 1838. By the 1890s, women were permitted to graduate from Scottish universities.

The revival of the European Diaconate did not originate, however, in Scotland. Theodor Fliedner, a German Lutheran minister, had visited Britain to raise funds for the poor in his parish and had seen the work of Elizabeth Fry. On his return to Germany he, too, began work in the prisons and he and his wife, Friederike, set up the first refuge for women released from prison, in a small house in their own garden. They also started a kindergarten and a course for teachers. This led on to Fliedner buying a house in the market place in Kaiserswerth and in 1836 to open there the first protestant hospital with a nursing school: the institution became the first Deaconess Motherhouse, and Theodor and Friederike called their nurses 'Deaconesses'.

Theodor wanted to renew the apostolic ministry of the Deaconess and to adapt it for a new time. He based it on the texts concerning women in the book of Acts and in the New Testament Epistles, as well as on reports of Deaconesses in the early Church. He had been impressed by the Moravians who had established the office of Deaconesses to perform a spiritual service by caring for sick and needy people, and also by the Catholic Sisters of Mercy who did not live in the cloister but also worked with needy people. Fliedner recognised the abilities of women and provided them with a professional education to nurse the sick and work amongst the poor. In the Motherhouse, Deaconess training and spiritual formation were developed by a style of life involving belief, service and living in community. They were single women and he wanted them to be respected in society and so they were given the dress and type of bonnet a married woman would wear: Friederike was head Sister of the Motherhouse. The Flieders' basic rule regulated the structure, life and service of all the houses of the Kaiserswerth tradition. Other ministers of the same theological persuasion also began institutions at places like Bielefeld under the direction of Bodelschwingh and at Neuendettelsau under Wilhelm Lohe. Johann Hinrich Wichern began work amongst the poor in a home: his Rauhes Haus. He trained young men to be brothers to the children in the home and to live together with them. It was the first Deacons' training in Germany although Wichern never called them Deacons. At a meeting in 1848 he called the Church Assembly to care for the poor and people in need. The work set up in the Inner Missions is now the European Federation for Diaconia.

Fliedner travelled to seek funds for his work and before long he had a number of buildings from which Diaconal work was carried out. He went to America and Jerusalem taking Deaconesses with him, establishing work and communities and so the European revival of the Diaconate was to spread around the world. In 1856 Florence Nightingale visited Kaiserswerth and on her return was to go on to set up a school for nurses in 1860. The early institutions then established are now major communities of care incorporating hospitals; social care of mentally and physical handicapped people; care of the elderly, and schools for children.

In 1856, when asked to present to the General Synod of Prussia (the largest Protestant Church) a paper on the place of the Diaconate in the church, Fliedner and Wichern demanded that Diakonia should be recognised as a regular ministry. However the Synod did not follow their ideas to establish the Diaconate in the church. On the 150th anniversary questions were still being asked if the Diaconate would become an established ministry in the Evangelical Church.

There were many similarities between Archibald and Catherine Charteris and Theodor and Friederike Fliedner. Both couples were involved in work reaching out to the poor. As a parish minister Charteris had encouraged his wealthy congregation in the Park Church to work among the poorer people in the downtown area of Port Dundas in Glasgow. When he moved to Edinburgh as Professor of Biblical Studies he began an outreach programme from the Tolbooth Church with a team of students and others to work in the poorer areas of the city. His wife Catherine helped to lead a band of women who ministered to the women and children in the deprived slum area.

Charteris with his friend Major the Hon. Robert Baillie persuaded the 1869 General Assembly of the Church of Scotland to appoint a committee to inquire into Christian work in the country. They believed there was a vast dormant power among the laity, and among women in particular, who could assist ministers. Charteris requested that he be Convener of this Committee. The Christian Life and Work Committee was formed and it continued until 1936. He himself was Convener for 25 years. Questionnaires were sent out to the Church and information was gathered on evangelistic efforts, congregational activity, what was happening in family worship, prayer meetings, Sunday schools and Bible class, and outreach to groups such as the fisher-folk, domestic servants, farm labourers. In particular the work of women in the church was investigated. Women's work for Foreign Missions had been regulated by the Assembly but Charteris challenged the Church also to consider regulating women's work within the Church in Scotland. The big question for Charteris was: 'What did the Church need for the present time?' He explored the possible restoration of the order of Deaconess in the Church both by visiting the institutions on the continent and by looking at the documents of the ancient Church.

REV. PROFESSOR CHARTERIS, D.D.

In his Baird lecture in 1877 Charteris traced the recognition of women's work back to the time of Phoebe (Romans 16: 1). He quoted the prayer at the solemn service for the ordination of a Deaconess in the so–called 'Apostolic Constitutions' [c.380 AD]. He considered how the work had flourished in the Eastern Church longer than it had done in the West. Deaconesses had been used to give instruction to the female catechumens and were present at baptism: their role in the church was often described as gate-keeper. Charteris believed that while Deaconesses were part of the organisation of the Apostolic Church, with the growth of monasticism the female ministry found in Scripture had eventually been abolished. The Deaconess of the early Church had differed fundamentally from the nun but the latter had supplanted her. A plausible reason to account for this supposed past error had been found in the Synod of Epaone [517 AD]. *'The Diaconate was too free an order of too miscellaneous usefulness to be under the dominion of men; and so it disappeared'*.[iii]

Charteris was not content with historical research; he had gone himself to view the work being done by Fliedner at Kaiserswerth and also work carried out by Deaconesses in their hospital in Egypt. He visited organisations like the Mildmay Institutions, Dr Barnardo's Homes and the London Bible Women's Mission: he met with Deaconesses of the Manchester City Mission. He studied German, French and Swiss Diaconal institutions. However in his Baird lecture Charteris argued that the institutions on the continent were founded by individuals and were not Church institutions: their Deaconesses were responsible to the various independent committees and not to the Church or denominational authorities. Although the trained nurses and teachers of Europe were models and pioneers, for him, they were not Deaconesses as in the early Church. The Deaconesses at Kaiserswerth were responsible to Pastor Fliedner and his successors. While they were Deaconesses in the sense of ministering to the poor as Christ himself did, they were not in an office as in the early Church.[iv] In their work they cooperated with the Church but were under the authority of the institution. Similar things could be said of the Mildmay Deaconesses, Dr Barnardo's and the Sisterhoods of the Church of England and others. Charteris said, '*If women were*

11

to be part of the Corporate Church they must be subject to it and owe to it their standing and power'.[v] For him it followed that if women were officials of the Church they also had the right to ordination from the Church. He thought if there was need for the ministries of women then that was sufficient reason to ordain them to discharge their ministry. So when Charteris brought his scheme for the office of Deaconess to the General Assembly it was his intention that they be ordained by Presbytery.

Following the General Assembly of 1877, questionnaires were sent to seek the opinions of the Church. While some opposed the formal organisation of women's work there was a general consensus that there was a need for a training Institute to train people for work both at Home and Overseas, and for the revival of the ancient and scriptural office of Deaconess.[vi] A suggestion was made by the minister of St Giles in Edinburgh that there should be a Deaconess House and that *'the ladies should devote themselves entirely to Christian work in parishes with the consent of the minister'*. He recommended that a badge should be worn when on duty. Opinion in the Church was divided as to whether more than one category of women workers should be recognised but there was unanimity of the fact that the women working in the parish should be *'duly trained by the church'*.[vii]

Charteris as convener of the Christian Life and Work Committee brought his proposals to the General Assembly of 1886 with the view that the Deaconess in the Church of Scotland would be at the pinnacle of a pyramid of women's work in the Church. *The Scotsman*, 26 May 1886, reported that the idea of women being recognised by the Church was received with much hilarity.[viii] The Committee, however, proposed regulations for training Deaconesses and for women who would work in Foreign Missions. There were to be two classes of Deaconesses: those who would have had two years training in the training institution, and those whose qualifications had been attested by their work in their home congregations over a period of no less than seven years. Everyone in training was to receive practical training in parochial work under the guidance of ministers and Kirk Sessions.[ix]

When Charteris proposed to the 1887 Assembly that women who had the approved qualifications be set apart as Deaconesses, his intention was that they would be ordained to the office by Presbytery and would be subject to the minister and Kirk Session of the Parish. Arthur Gordon, in his biography of Charteris, says '*The scheme had an all too easy passage through the Assembly and in the following autumn a breeze occurred in Edinburgh Presbytery, which slightly checked the movement. Dr Phin took exception to what seemed like putting the deaconesses above the elder if she were set apart by the Presbytery*'.[x] The Christian Life and Work Committee itself was divided in its opinion and the following year submitted an alternative set of regulations to the Assembly giving them the option of the Deaconess being set apart by the Kirk Session rather than set apart or ordained by Presbytery. The Kirk Session route was what the Assembly chose. It was to be another 104 years before Deacons were fully integrated into the courts of the church and 114 years before they were ordained to their office.

The first Deaconess, Lady Grisell Baillie, was set apart in Bowden Kirk on 9 December 1888. Alice Maxwell and Catherine Davidson were set apart on 13 January 1889 in St Cuthbert's Church, Edinburgh. They were allowed to put DCS (Deaconess of the Church of Scotland) after their names giving a form of recognition of their office and an identity.

3

The Early Years

'...............I am among you as one who serves' (Lk22;27b)

Over the next ten years the numbers of Deaconesses slowly increased in the established Church, and reports were enthusiastic. In the 1891 report to the General Assembly on the small band of Deaconesses, the proverb was quoted *'that small beginnings have often great endings'* expressing the hope that the work would spread as the value of the services of Deaconesses became known. The 'band' over the years has remained small and although some know the value of the work undertaken by the Diaconate, still the hope is that as the work becomes yet better known more will realise the value of the office of Deacon in the Church.

Many of the early Deaconesses were women of independent means and worked *'at their own charge'*, as it was described, paying for their own training at Deaconess House. Hence until recent times there was never a budget specifically for training Deaconesses: and this, later, led to the difficulties. Most were single women in the age range of 30 to 60 and reflected the social pattern of the age, of single women entering on charitable work. Some were widows and special consideration was given to daughters of ministers who it was thought would be suitably qualified to enter the work.

Training at the Institute covered such topics as 'Methods and Practice of Home Mission', 'Medical Hygiene for District Visitors', 'Scripture Knowledge' and the 'Art of Teaching', 'Practical Training in the Work of District Visiting' and 'History and Methods of Mission to the Heathen'. As well as training in what was to become the Deaconess House, it was also carried out at the St Ninian's Training Mission which was later to become the Missionary Training Institution for the Church. Practical work was carried out there and in the Pleasance district of Edinburgh, where pastoral needs were entrusted to the care of Deaconess House and its 'Brown Ladies' as they were called. Brown had been chosen as the Church of Scotland Deaconess dress. It was neat and serviceable and the dress was recognised in the community. For outdoor use there was a brown bonnet, cloak or cape. For indoor use there was a white muslin cap with brown ribbon and a muslin apron.

Collaborative working was involved from the start as those training to be Deaconesses worked with divinity students from the University Missionary Association comparing notes, meeting fortnightly with the men and discussing experiences of visiting in the area. Practice and theory were held together; visits were recorded and later discussed. It was seen as essential that principles were learned and put into practice in assisting in the various groups, such as the Band of Hope, Mothers' Meetings, Sewing Classes and Kitchen Meetings. Training was also offered to students of both the Women's Foreign Mission and the Women's Association for Home Mission.

Poverty meant poor health and in a day prior to National Health Services the Deaconess was called on to help with sick nursing. A home was opened in Glasgow and residents were given nurse training at the Royal Infirmary in Glasgow. Nursing was thus considered an important part of Deaconess preparation and lack of adequate facilities for this convinced the Committee of the need for a hospital connected to the Deaconess House. It would have the dual purpose of benefiting the sick and training the Deaconess for such nursing as she would require in carrying out her duties in the parishes of Scotland, besides assisting those going abroad to work in the mission field. A site for the Deaconess Hospital was procured next to the St Ninian's Training Institute. Some Deaconesses became fully qualified nurses and worked as hospital staff, other went overseas while others were trained to meet the needs of simple emergencies in the Parish.

Another development came in the form of a request from Edinburgh's Calton Prison for a Chaplain and Miss Anderson DCS was appointed. Further, in 1898 an orphanage was opened at Queensferry when an institution founded 24 years previously by Dr

William Robertson was relocated. On Robertson's death his daughter Gertrude Robertson DCS had succeeded him. From the opening at Queensferry the orphanage was placed under the care of Miss K. Davidson DCS until she had to leave at the end of the year because of family circumstances. It then came under the direction of Annie Sanderson DCS. Fourteen children were admitted in the first year. Moreover the Christian Life and Work Committee also took on the Home House for Missionaries' children at Duddingston which was run by Miss Minnie Paterson DCS and her sister.

For some years there had been an idea of a house of rest for elderly or invalid Deaconesses. The house was opened at Appin Lodge, Dalkeith. Some mission workers had breakdowns through over strain. Part of this was due to the solitariness of their work and living in lodgings. One of the purposes of the house was to provide a place for workers who required a week or fortnight's holiday. The Deaconess Rest Home also served the needs of those who returned from the mission field and after a few years it was extended to others too.

The first Conference for Deaconesses was set up by Charteris in 1894 for the 'deepening of the spiritual life'. The opportunity to come together and share experiences was much appreciated by the Deaconesses and it has remained an important aspect of the Diaconate today in the form of Diaconate Council. In his closing address at the Conference, Charteris said the ministry of the Diaconate was one of service following the example of Jesus Christ who came not to be served but to serve. (Matthew 20: 28) In the address he said the German method of subjecting the Deaconesses to a stricter than military rule, with men at the head of the governing body, had been adopted in Europe to prevent contention arising. To Charteris, however, it seemed that Fliedner and his followers had sacrificed individuality in order to secure unity, whereas in the Church of Scotland they were trying to maintain greater freedom for each one. There were certain things he wished to impress on them. First, that they were pioneers of a great advance in the Church of Christ. It was the first attempt by a protestant Church to appoint the female Diaconate to the responsible posts to which they were called.

Second, the work to which they were called was to be their life: not something added on, but their vocation. Third, they were to be beware of ambition: their life was to be one of self denial so that others seeing their good works would glorify God. Fourth, they were to try to make the best of where they were and not to alter things for their 'own notions'. He stressed the importance of being content where they were because that was where they were needed. Fifth, they were always to remember the words of Jesus '*Lo I am with you always*'. He emphasised the importance of Christian fellowship such as the Conference. He closed with the words of William Carey, the Baptist missionary: '*Expect great things from God, do great things for God*'.

In 1897 the General Assembly received proposals for a Deaconess Board which would report to the Christian Life and Work Committee. The Board would be responsible for caring for Deaconesses, securing employment, negotiating salaries and dealing with requests for placements and transfers. While as a Deaconess and a member of an order she would thus be under the authority of the Board, if employed by another Committee of the Church she would also be accountable to them. Over the years this dual responsibility has proved to be a tension between employing Committees and the Diaconate.

Around the same time Charteris' Life and Work Committee was expressing concern that there was an impression in the Church that there was no opening for women's work except in parishes. It emphasised that it never been the intention that Deaconesses would serve only in parishes carrying out pastoral work but would be in special positions of responsibility using their leadership and organisational skills. The Deaconess was someone approved by the Courts of the Church and recognised as having been trained for an office in the Church. The report of the Christian Life and Work Committee in 1906 stated that the Church could be '*proud of those whom it has ordained to sacred office*'.

Archibald Charteris' original vision had taken root in the Church by the time he died in 1908. By 1910 there were 52 Church of Scotland

Deaconesses: ten of them working overseas, 15 in Home Mission and 16 giving various kinds of service under the Christian Life and Work Committee. The work ranged from Superintendent of Deaconess House and placements in the Deaconess Hospital to overseas work – at Poona in India, in Egypt and Smyrna – as well as in a variety of parishes. Some were employed as Deputies who served as '*ministering angels*' to the girls who followed the fishing fleet from Barra and Shetland and Aberdeen to Yarmouth. They would bind up their hands, wounded when gutting the fish, as well as attending to their spiritual needs. Seven Deaconesses were set apart during the First World War and in 1916 a request was received from the Ministry of Munitions for Deaconesses to preside over the hostels provided for the women working in the munitions factories. Although numbers in training in the twenties was restricted, 22 Deaconesses were set apart from 1919 to 1929. Those who served as Deaconesses of the (established) Church of Scotland in the succession embodying Charteris' vision were known, from the colour of their uniform dress, as '*The Brown Deaconesses*'.

4

The Brown Deaconesses

'Jesus ... taking a towel ... poured water into a basin and began to wash his disciples' feet....'
(John 13: 4-5)

Lady Grisell Baillie

Lady Grisell Baillie, the first Deaconess, was set apart in Bowden Kirk. Born in Mellerstain, 1822, she was the youngest daughter in a family of eleven. She was brought up in a home filled with Christian love and devotion. Committing herself to God she found her brother Robert had also committed himself to God and the two worked closely together.

An elder in the church, Major Robert Baillie became one of the prime movers in the Christian Life and Work Committee. Lady Grisell and her brother were involved in pastoral work in the community. Her life of unwearied activity was guided by prayer as she and her brother the Major went on their work of mercy. For almost 50 years Lady Grisell had taught in the Sunday School at Bowden. She was also interested in overseas mission, promoting an annual sale to help fund the Zenana Mission. She set up a branch of the YWCA as well as providing the means to build a bridge over the Tweed. In the summer of 1888 her brother the Major died. Within a month of his death she had resumed teaching in Sunday School and visiting the parishioners in his elder's district.

On Sunday 9 December 1888 Lady Grisell was solemnly set apart as a Church of Scotland Deaconess in the Parish Church of Bowden. The minister, Dr Allardyce, conducted the service.

After her service Lady Grisell who was in her 67th year sent a very moving letter to Dr Charteris telling him about the service of setting her apart as the first Deaconess. She described the simple and moving ceremony as 'her wedding day'. She was extremely happy at being permitted to commit herself afresh to the work of the church. After her setting apart Lady Grisell was involved in the building of a Hall at Newton St Boswells in memory of her brother. In July of 1889 her second brother, Admiral Thomas Baillie, died. After a few weeks she was back continuing her work of holding Mothers' Meetings in the hall, providing books and magazines for people to read, teaching in the Sunday School at Bowden, visiting the poor.

Lady Grisell was an eloquent speaker. Her prayers at the Mothers' Meetings were described as 'most affecting and beautiful' and it is said she often wept over the folk she prayed for. When the first Conference of the Woman's Guild was held in Edinburgh in November 1891, it fell to Lady Grisell as first Deaconess of the Church to take the chair. A fortnight after her return from Edinburgh, however, she caught influenza from which she never recovered and was buried on Christmas Eve.

Katherine Davidson

On 13 January 1889 Katherine Davison was set apart in St Cuthbert's Church which was the Parish Church of the poor and densely populated area of the Pleasance district of Edinburgh's Royal Mile. Katherine Davidson had been acting as temporary Superintendent of Deaconess House until Alice Maxwell was able to take up the appointment. Katherine had previously worked at the Mildmay Deaconess Institution: she was to go on to be roving ambassador for the Woman's Guild, building up enthusiasm for the newly formed organisation.

She was later to be the first Deaconess appointed as Depute to the fisher-girls, following the herring fleet and ministering to the fisher-girls of Scotland, tending to their spiritual and physical needs around the British coast. She was to undertake direction of the work done by the lady Deputies. They travelled from Baltasound in Shetland to Scarborough, Lowestoft and Yarmouth. They would befriend the girls, visiting among them, skilfully dressing their cut fingers. At Baltasound, where she felt her lodging was too far away from the girls, she screened off a portion of the Mission Church and made her home there so that she could be in the midst of her people and they could find her by day or night. An article in the *Daily Telegraph* on the work at Lowestoft and Yarmouth described how Miss Davidson was there to meet the girls when they arrived at the start of a new season, with tea spread out for them. The season lasted six to eight weeks. At Yarmouth she provided the rest house for Scottish fisher folk at a cost of £500 to herself. In one year they received 8,355 visits from the girls, and ministered to 544 patients who needed 920 hand-dressings. In the rest house they served 1,100 breakfasts and 3,452 dinners to say nothing of the endless cups of tea, meals being provided at nominal prices. The work was carried out ecumenically, help being given by the United Free Church, the Methodist and Independent Churches.

Alice Maxwell

MISS ALICE MAXWELL, D.C.S.,
FIRST SUPERINTENDENT OF THE DEACONESS HOUSE.

Alice Maxwell, who also was set part on 13 January 1889 in St Cuthbert's Church, had been recommended to Charteris by her parish minister at Anwoth as the person to run Deaconess House and the training Institution. The youngest daughter of Sir William Maxwell of Cardoness, she was an unlikely choice as her health was not robust and she did not see herself as worthy to take on the task. She reluctantly agreed to take on the role on condition that she be given time to prepare both physically and mentally. She spent time in Australia and on her return spent time at the Mildmay and Rochester Deaconess Institutions as well as the Orphanage of Mercy at Kilburn. She was to prove to be an inspired choice as Superintendent of Deaconess House going on to train Deaconesses and initiating practical mission work to the poor for 23 years.

Deaconess House was founded to be a home as well as a training institution for ministers' daughters and other '*well–bred young women*' who would train for missionary work. The first Deaconess House opened its doors at 33 Mayfield Gardens, moving the following year to 41 George Square before settling in 27 George Square in 1890.

As Superintendent, Alice Maxwell was to set the pattern for training, holding studies and practical work together as well as training students for work both at home and overseas. The programme was varied and lectures were given by ministers from both Edinburgh and country parishes. Practical work was carried out in the Sunday Schools, visiting the sick, Mothers' Meetings, Temperance work, and introducing medical hygiene. Temperance Meetings started at 7pm and finished at 10pm when the pubs were closed. 'Sunday Home', held in St Ninian's Training Institute, was held between 2:30pm and 5:30pm for poor children, who had a time of teaching followed by games between 4 and 5pm; and tea, bread and jam was served before they returned home. Sunday was a full day for Alice Maxwell's students, finishing after the evening service with prayers, led by the workers, for all that had happened throughout the day.

Weekdays at George Square began with breakfast at 8:30am and prayers at nine. Prayers were short but with a quiet, simple reverence that brought God close to the students. It gave them an understanding of the deep and meaningful power of prayer. It was said that Alice Maxwell's prayers brought people near the presence of God. One mother in the Pleasance said, '*When Miss Maxwell says a prayer you just ken she is awfu' friends wi God*'.[xi] In spite of her days being very full, she always had time for students who came to her to talk over their difficulties. Mornings at the house were devoted to study and afternoons and evenings to district visiting and meetings.

Miss Maxwell had great interest in the General Assembly and was seldom absent from her seat in the gallery when the reports of Foreign Mission, Home Mission, Christian Life and Work, Temperance and the Social schemes of the Church were given. Each year she reported to the Assembly through the Christian Life and Work Committee on the work of the Deaconess House. She also reported the work of the House (and later of the Deaconess Hospital) at the Woman's Guild Annual Meeting. Her addresses were inspiring and challenging.

When the first official Health Visitors were appointed in Edinburgh in 1908, Miss Maxwell took an active part in the scheme; and, similarly, when the 1910 World Missionary Conference was held in Edinburgh she attended sessions as much as she could although by this time her health was failing. In 1911 she gave her last report to the Guild Conference. It was with great sorrow that the Guilds-women heard of her resignation and warmly passed a resolution expressing thanks for all the service she had rendered over her twenty three years at Deaconess House.

Alice Maxwell's death four years later, on 15 February 1915, brought many tributes from those who worked with her. *'Her work must ever remain a fragrant memory with those who were trained under her. Her capacity for taking pains over the smallest detail influenced us. She took endless trouble in training her students, and was keen to mark improvement in those she trained'*. Yet another wrote:[xii] *'We, her sister Deaconesses, feel that the first chapter in the History of the Diaconate of the Church of Scotland is finished. It remains for us to write a second that will be worthy of its noble beginning'*.

Katherine Rae

Katherine Rae was one of two ladies set apart as Deaconesses in the Tron Kirk, Edinburgh, on 22 May 1898. She was 44, and was appointed to a parish in Alexandria, Dumbarton in 1898. On 7 May 1902 she was appointed to St Clement's Church, in Govan, Glasgow. There she served for seven years before being appointed in 1909 to serve as Superintendent of Deaconess House in Belfast, and to be involved in the development of training of Deaconesses in the Presbyterian Church in Ireland. Arrangements were made for the Deaconess Hospital in Edinburgh to provide hospital training for them. However owing to the small numbers going forward, the training was transferred to Edinburgh in the 1920s and their students were to continue to train at St Colm's until the 1990s. On her return from Belfast Katherine was appointed as Superintendent of the Probationers' Home in connection with the Women's Association for

Home Missions in Glasgow in 1912. She was to remain there until her retiral in 1921 which would have made her 71.

Isabella (Bell) Kesting

On 10 March 1895, Isabella (Bell) Kesting DCS was set apart at the St Ninian's Mission Hall of St Cuthbert's Parish Church, Edinburgh. She served as a missionary in Poona, India, until 1908 when she returned home on sick leave. She worked for a time at the Deaconess Hospital before returning to Poona in 1911. From 1914 she again served at Deaconess House before being appointed to St Leonard's Parish, Edinburgh, from 1915 to 1933. A poem about her was written by a young woman in her parish:

> The trig wee bunnet broon a 'ween
> Enframed a sympathetic face
> A' lichted up wi' heavenly grace;
> The kinlee een, steadfast, serene
> She aften luiked thru the specs
> On sichts that sadden sair an vex
> Tireless she flitted up and doon
> The back stairs o'oor auld grey toon
> A ministerin' angel; wooed
> The hapless folk she dearly looed;
> Into our joys and sorrows cam'an.
> Cheerin' the lonely wi' a psalm;
> Hertenin' the warkless in the strife
> Guidin' the weans in the way o' life;
> Easin' the weary o'their load,
> Pittin' the auld in the care o' God.

Minnie Mullo Weir

Minnie Mullo Weir DCS, was the youngest of five children. She was born in Joppa, Portobello. From an early age she wanted to work for the Church. Her three brothers were ministers and trained at Edinburgh University where she herself studied for an MA in English, History and French. Her sister was a teacher. Between 1913 and 1930 there was thus a Mullo Weir at the University and one of her tutors enquired as to whether there were any more Mullo Weirs to come! On leaving University Minnie went on to take a one year teacher training course at Moray House followed by a one year training between Deaconess House and St Colm's College. She was set apart as a Deaconess on 24 June 1934 in Corstorphine Old, Edinburgh, and was appointed to Wallacetown in Dundee where she served for two years.

It was a time of economic depression and her work in Dundee was very much amongst the women and children. In one home she visited, the husband was ill. Each time she visited the wife she saw the husband who as a result of her regular visits became a member of the Church of Scotland.

Minnie served two years in Dundee before returning to Edinburgh to look after her mother for twenty years. During this time she was involved in the Church on a voluntary basis: whether at St Cuthbert's, speaking at women's meetings for various churches in Edinburgh, and taking meetings at New College Settlement. Sometimes she could convene up to 37 meetings a year.

In 1958 she worked at the Church of Scotland's Mission at Great Yarmouth. Occasionally she would have to make her way over the boats to reach some of the fishermen. The mission cat always followed her on her visits! Her next posting came in 1959, when she was appointed to Templehall, Kirkcaldy, Fife, where the work was very different from her days in Dundee – there were 1000 children in the Sunday School.

Minnie Mullo Weir served for four years as one of the two Deaconess representatives on the Council of the Association of Women Workers after it was formed in 1940. This was a group which sought to bring together the two branches of women's work then supported by the Church of Scotland, the Church Sisters and the Deaconesses. She served on this group until the time when there were further discussions regarding the Order of Deaconesses and other women workers in the Church. By then she could not see any need for separation of the two groups as the training and the work was very similar.

A small birdlike figure with a keen sense of humour, Minnie Mullo Weir retired on 3 August 1966. In her lifetime Minnie had seen many changes and could remember reading about the Suffragettes. She was very alert and interested in all that was going on until the last few years: surely it was only her failing sight which prevented her learning about computers. Even her failing sight did not prevent her from writing her own Christmas cards until she was 102. Her writing was small and precise. When she finally succumbed to going into a residential home she didn't like to sit in the lounge where the '*old folk just sat and nodded*'. As she grew increasingly frailer she would say, '*You can live too long*'. Her philosophy for whatever was happening was to say, '*It will pass*'. Although her body was physically frail her mind was sharp. Minnie died on 20 July 2010 in her 105th year.

Phyllis Bain

Phyllis Bain was one of the last Deaconesses to be commissioned under the Order of Deaconesses (Brown Deaconesses) in 1943. She served for 26 years in St Cuthbert's Church in Edinburgh where she was greatly loved and valued, and then for eight years as Hospital Chaplain's Assistant in Edinburgh Royal Infirmary.

5

Deaconess Nurses and The Deaconess Hospital

'When did we ever see you sick or in prison and visit you?'
(Matthew 25: 39)

The Deaconess Hospital was opened 11 October 1894 with Miss Ella Pirie appointed as Deaconess Superintendent. It was the first hospital founded as an integral part of the organisation of a protestant Church. The object of the hospital was to give training in sick nursing to women who were to be involved in Home Mission work and also to those going overseas. It was built as a memorial to Lady Grisell Baillie and was designed to complete the

MISSION HALL AND DEACONESS HOSPITAL.

education of Christian workers, especially Church Deaconesses. It was not the primary intention to train a professional sick nurse but rather a year's training was considered sufficient to help the poor in their own homes. However the hospital did offer opportunities to anyone who wished to be a professional nurse. There was to be a special sub-division of the Diaconate who would be known as Deaconess Nurses. As well as the nursing side they were trained to give care to people spiritually without proselytising, learning to unite care of the body with healing of the soul when engaged as Parish Deaconesses or as foreign missionaries. Services were conducted on a Sunday with morning and evening prayers daily. Miss Robertson DCS went in to read and talk with the patients one day a week.

The Deaconess Hospital was opened at a total cost of £3,716. Later an adjacent building was acquired to make the hospital a centre for the training of district nurses as well as to provide room for surgical treatment. Cost of a bed in the hospital for a year was £40. Some beds were supported by Guilds or individuals. It had 22 beds spread over three wards, one of which was an isolation ward with two beds.

MISS ELLA PIRRIE, D.C.S.,
FIRST MATRON OF THE DEACONESS HOSPITAL.

Ella Pirie DCS was to be the only Deaconess to be Superintendent of the hospital. Ella had been nursing in Liverpool and had a wide experience in England, Germany and Ireland. She was set apart as a Deaconess on 10 March 1895 in St Ninian's Mission; Elizabeth Buchanan and Isabella Kesting, probationers, and Annie Sanderson were ordained at the same time. It is reported Ella gave her services without any salary. She came to the Church at the time the hospital was being built and had experience in sick nursing and hospital management. The hospital was planned and initiated under her wise guidance. She sought to foster a missionary spirit within the hospital keeping in mind the purpose for which it was built. Her bright and attractive personality, her unselfish disposition, and her kindly thoughtfulness for others won her the affection of her sister Deaconesses and fellow workers. Her whole heart was in the Diaconate and its work. She retired from the hospital in 1914 but continued to serve as Superintendent of the Deaconess Rest Home.

District nursing was begun by the Deaconess Superintendent in 1896. There were rules set about the number of hours spent visiting in a day. Reports of those visited and number of times visited were recorded in a book and presented to the Superintendent weekly. Referrals came from the Deaconesses working in the St Ninian's district.

In the Assembly report of the Life and Work Committee of 1896 it was noted there had been requests from three parishes for a Deaconess Nurse, but at that time there was no one available with the necessary qualifications. The following year it was reported that Miss Jane Paton DCS who had served in the Canongate and in Abbey Parish, Paisley, had been appointed to take charge of the district nursing in the Pleasance district in connection with the Deaconess Hospital. A report on the work in 1898 said that 250 cases were attended by her and her probationer assistants with a total of 1,384 visits paid. The work grew steadily over the years. It was reported as being '*of value for its own sake but also provided excellent training for the probationer Deaconesses*'. They contacted people who were considered unsuitable to admit to the hospital: some were suffering from an incurable illness, some were patients who could not leave their own homes; as well as seeing many minor ailments. Miss Paton described their work in an account to a Woman's Guild Assembly as not always being a pleasant experience but of great benefit to the patients whose needs were attended to: food and clothing being given as well as medicine, sympathy and care.

Mary McCartney DCS served as a Deaconess Nurse in Portree. She was paid by the Women's Home Mission Committee, by the United Free Church of Scotland and by the Portree Nursing Association. She saw herself as someone the poor could turn to without having to call for a doctor. Kate Collins DCS was set apart as a Deaconess in St Michael's Church, Edinburgh, in 1907, serving first in the Canongate and then as a Staff Nurse in the Deaconess Hospital. In 1912 she was appointed as Deaconess Nurse to the Parish of St Mary's, Dundee, where she was to serve for 24 years until her retirement.

All of this was prior to the National Health Service. With the introduction of the NHS the Deaconess Nursing service passed out of the Church's jurisdiction.

6

Ministry to the Poor

'When Lord did we ever see you hungry and fed you ... naked and clothed you?'
(Matthew 25: 37-38)

The story of the early years of the Diaconate would not be complete without including a section on the Parish Sisters of the Church of Scotland and the Church Sisters of the United Free Church of Scotland. Individuals whose service began with both these groupings were latterly part of the Diaconate as we know it today. (Yet another stream of service, with its own origins also in the missionary movement of the 19th century, in later years became a constituent part of the current Diaconate: the men recognised as Lay Missionaries. These, however, have had their own story told already.[xiii])

In 1893 the Home Mission Committee of the established Church proposed a Women's Association for Home Missions. The following year the Committee advised that all '*poor parishes*' should have '*a sister of mercy who would manifest to the weary and heavy laden the tenderness of a woman's care*'. The need of woman workers who could go to the homes of the poor and sick was thus identified for the poorest parishes which could least afford it, and so the Home Mission Committee sought to supply the need by recruiting and training for the new post of Parish Sister – in addition, this is, to those ladies being set aside as Deaconesses via Archibald Charteris' Committee on Christian Life and Work. Two committees of the General Assembly were therefore offering separate routes for women to serve in the Church. In setting up their new group the Home Mission Committee said, '*They were conscious of the inadvisability of adding a new association but they felt it was absolutely necessary*'.[xiv] By 1895 the Women's Association were raising funds to support five Parish Sisters and give grants towards the salaries of four more.

Early reports show how Parish Sisters in town churches were supported by rural areas. Practical help was given by work parties of the Woman's Guild sending clothing and other items to be given out by the Sisters. Most Parish Sisters worked in Edinburgh, Glasgow, and the mining areas in the Central Belt. Numbers gradually increased in the parishes and more Parish Sisters could have been employed through Home Mission if funds had been available. By the fifth year 235 of the 1,370 parishes in Scotland were assisting in the work of 24 Parish Sisters, five of whom were also Deaconesses. More affluent parishes provided whole or part of the salary of those in the poorer city areas. The Committee appealed to '*ladies of education and leisure*' to train for Mission Service at home particularly if they were unable to devote themselves to foreign mission. Training consisted of six months in Deaconess House and Hospital.

The Parish Sisters acted as Christian missionaries to the poor and helped with the Temperance movement. They served soup, provided other material aid to the poor and assisted in getting help from charitable societies. They would conduct Mothers' meetings or sewing classes for girls, Boys Clubs, coal and clothing clubs, as well as evenings with the Woman's Guild with demonstrations in cookery and nursing. Daily journals of work undertaken were submitted to the minister monthly and to the Committee six monthly. One report from a Parish Sister working in Dundee said that she had 240 names on her visiting list, which including the sick, the poor, young married women whose church attendance was irregular and those who were not members of any church. She also had a special interest in factory girls, especially those who lived in lodgings or in a house of their own. She assisted at four different meetings held weekly for the poor or for factory girls.

In 1912 a Mission House was opened in Glasgow where probationers were able to get further practical work before taking on the responsibilities of a Parish Sister. The flat was set up at 34 Lawrence

St. in Glasgow and had accommodation for three residents and a Superintendent. Miss Katherine Rae DCS was appointed as Superintendent and was well qualified for this task. Students acquired knowledge of different branches of parochial work in The Barony and Govan as well as the Medical Mission, Lodging Houses and Charity Organisation Society. They were to spend six months in the house after their training at Deaconess House. This had the duel purpose of increasing their confidence and enabling the Committee to know their capabilities. Lady Pearce had generously given a large Institute in Govan to be used for the people of the parish and the top flat was able to be used by the students.

By 1915 the war crisis was affecting the work of the Parish Sisters. Women became involved in war work and were not going forward for training. In the summer of 1916 a request was received for matrons for the hostels in a large munitions factory at Gretna. The Mission Committee arranged with the United Free Church to share in the work in the area, which went ahead under the direction of Miss Hannah DCS who worked for the Women's Association of Home Mission. It was said she made a '*very honoured place for herself in the community*'. She had the help of a Mrs Steven, a Church Sister of the United Free Church..

Few people went forward for training in the war years but by 1919 it was hoped that numbers would increase with the recruitment of women leaving their wartime duties. However that was not to be the case and even during the twenties numbers going forward to train were small. This may have been due to the fact that the role of women in society was changing. There were many firsts in the 1920s of women taking a professional role in society. Nevertheless there were 45 Church of Scotland Parish Sisters, 16 of whom were Deaconesses. At this time monthly services were held in St Cuthbert's, Edinburgh, and The Barony, Glasgow, for the purpose of putting workers in touch with each other and with members of the Committee.

Another strand of the development of the Diaconate was through the Church Sisters introduced into the United Free Church of Scotland in

1916. The work they carried out was similar to the Parish Sisters of the established Church: visiting the unchurched, the poor, the sick, working in Sunday School, Temperance work, work amongst the fisher-folk and the berry pickers. They did two years training at the UF Women's Missionary College or similar.

It would appear that in 1925 the United Free Church introduced the office of Deaconess whose work was to be similar to the Church Sisters but to have higher entrance qualifications. Training was to be at university degree level, following a similar course to that required for the ministry of Word and Sacrament. An additional session of study at the Women's Missionary College or Assembly training schools would also be required. UF Deaconesses were to be paid a salary of £180 whereas the Church Sister's salary was £120. A Church Sister could qualify as a Deaconess provided she had the required educational standard. There was, however, to be no further mention of the work of UF Deaconesses prior to the Union of the Churches in 1929.

One of the notable projects in the United Free Church at this time was the team of Church Sisters in Fife, based in Lochgelly and Cowdenbeath. They worked in the missions and cooperated with the work going on in the congregations, developing a collaborative ministry with the ministers. Much of the work was under the direction of Miss Craig. It included Sunday School training events and Guilds of Friendship for women. In 1927 they were represented on the Home Mission Committee of Dunfermline Presbytery.

In the mid-1920s both the Church of Scotland and the United Free Church of Scotland introduced a pension scheme for their Sisters.

In 1929 the Union took place between the Church of Scotland and the United Free Church of Scotland bringing together the 53 Parish Sisters and the 60 Church Sisters under the one title of Church Sisters, who were agents of the new, united Women's Home Mission Committee. There were 62 Deaconesses, of whom 19 worked as Parish Sisters.

The Order of Deaconesses was to remain.

7

After the Union of the Churches

'For everything its season and for every activity under heaven its time.'
(Ecclesiastes 3: 1)

With the Union of the Churches the administration of the United Church was arranged in departments, responsible to the various Committees of the General Assembly. The areas of women's work we have considered so far, the Brown Deaconesses, the Parish Sisters and the Church Sisters who became known as Church Sisters , continued to be organised by separate Committees.

The Home Mission Committee (soon renamed the Home Board) included the Women's Home Mission Association which was responsible for the Church Sisters appointed by their Committee, some of whom were Deaconesses. Regulations were agreed for the Church Sisters who were set apart at a public service. The Committee did not guarantee to provide work for those recognised as Church Sisters nor was it a lifelong appointment to the work. A Church Sister, as such, was *'an agent'* of the Women's Home Mission Committee but was not recognised as being in an office in the Church. They were required to have two years training at the (former United Free) Women's Missionary College: St Colm's, and at (the former established Church) Deaconess House; followed by a six month probation period. They worked in the industrial districts, new housing schemes and some country towns, and were involved with Play Centres and Clubs, Guildry and Guide Companies, Bible Classes and Girls' Associations. Some were also appointed to work with the berry pickers and the fisher-girls. The Church Sisters of the Women's Home Mission Committee wore a regulation grey uniform.

Meanwhile the Christian Life and Work Committee supervised the work of the Woman's Guild, the Deaconess House, the Deaconess Rest Home, the Deaconess Hospital and the Order of Deaconesses. At the Union, provisional regulations for the Order of Deaconesses were drawn up which offered a spiritual career for women, within limits, similar to the ministry for men. This spiritual ministry might be exercised in Home or in Foreign Mission and might include such positions as:

* Assistant to a minister in a congregation, with permission to preach;
* Principal of an Institution connected with the training for Women Students; or for social services or for the carrying on of preventive or rescue work among women;
* Superintendent of Home Mission work within a Presbytery or other large area;
* Organising Secretary or Deputy appointed by a Committee of the Church or as a leader employed in any sphere of social service;
* Doctor, nurse, lecturer, teacher or evangelist primarily in connection with the Church of Scotland;
* A sphere might also be found in Art, Music or Literature.

These regulations intended to place the Deaconesses in positions of leadership and responsibility: the proposal for Deaconesses to preach was a fairly radical proposal for the Church at that time however in society the 1920s had seen a number of professions open their doors to women. Women had received the vote in 1928.

Post-Union, women intending to become Deaconesses had to satisfy the Committee on Christian Life and Work of their suitability for acceptance as a candidate. While a university course was desirable it was not essential. The training was to be three years in St Ninian's and St Colm's. A shorter course was possible at St Colm's for those who already had a degree. Candidates had to be at least 21. Deaconesses were set apart to '*the office*'. The care and supervision of the Deaconesses was be under a Committee of 26 members who reported to the Assembly through the Life and Work Committee. On it were representatives from the various employing Committees and two from the Order of Deaconesses. This Committee was to be responsible for receiving applications and for arranging training. Those wishing to employ Deaconesses were to apply to the Committee, which would also direct and advise Deaconesses not under a Committee of the Church. Its remit was also to consider developments in the work of Deaconesses and to arrange study courses and retreats.

These two different groups – Women's Home Mission's Church Sisters, and Christian Life and Work's Deaconesses – thus operated under two different sets of regulations for three years following the Union.

In 1931 a petition was presented to the Assembly by the Marchioness of Aberdeen & Temair asking that the barriers preventing women entering the ministry, the eldership and the Diaconate be removed. A Committee was set up to look at the points raised in the petition. That same year, the Women's Home Mission Committee and the Committee on Christian Life and Work again brought regulations for their areas of work as instructed at the time of Union. The two sets of regulations highlighted the differences between the different cultures and traditions in existence and they were put into operation until a scheme could be brought which would bring together the service of the women in the Church. The regulations proposed by the Christian Life and Work Committee were the same as had been presented at the Union with the words '*permission to preach*' removed. The Committee was asked to reconsider and to report the following year. Although the 1931 proposals acknowledged the office of Deaconess as a spiritual order of ministry, in a leadership position, they stepped back from recommending she should be allowed to preach: suggesting it be considered by Presbyteries.

The Assembly approved the regulations and instructed that they continue until such time as a revised scheme could be brought which would bring the separate groups together. Over the next 60 years many schemes involving the Diaconate would be introduced and revised. The Committee charged with looking at the wider role of women in the Church recommended there should be further discussion; and that was also a journey which was to take 30 years although it was agreed women could be admitted as local congregational office-bearers, but not as elders.

By the late thirties the debate was on the place of the Order of Deaconesses in the Church as well as giving consideration to all fulltime women workers. There was a suggestion for a Sisterhood in the Church for all women workers, and within that Sisterhood, Deaconesses, who would be women with distinctive training or qualifications who were conscious of a vocation to service and spiritual leadership. Although it was acknowledged there was no longer a practical distinction between the work of a Deaconess and a Church Sister, it was nevertheless felt there was still a distinctive place for an Order of Deaconesses. It was once again proposed that the function of a Deaconess should include teaching and preaching particularly to woman and girls; and that those qualified should be ordained by Presbytery. The scheme was sent to Presbyteries and was revised to include preparation of first communicants and preparation of parents presenting children for baptism; but no mention was made of ordination. However it was to be into the seventies before Deaconesses were used in this way.

A joint Committee was set up to look at the Order of Deaconesses but meanwhile the early 1940s saw a Women's Association set up. There were on-going discussions regarding the difficulty of advancing the Order of Deaconesses when different employing Committees required different training. The Committees were also indifferent as to whether they employed Deaconesses as such or not. Questions were also raised regarding the relationship of women to the Courts of the Church and the fact they had no direct voice within the General Assembly.

There was confusion in people's minds regarding the existence of two separate groups of women workers in the Church when their functions and salaries were the same. The only difference was that Deaconesses required a higher standard of education than Church Sisters. It was felt the time was right for one Order, which would embrace all women workers in the Church. By 1945 the Deaconesses themselves questioned the need for an Order when there was no work which only they could do. Positions in which Deaconesses had previously served were being filled by otherwise qualified women; and parish work was carried out by Church Sisters. With dwindling numbers and the advancing age group of the Deaconesses, it was doubtful if the order had a future unless the situation was rectified. Three possible courses of action thus seemed open in the post-war years:

* To dissolve the Order or allow it to lapse for a period of years;
* To form a single Order, consisting of Deaconesses, Church Sisters and all women with a vocation to fulltime service in the Church, having undertaken a course of training;
* To distinguish clearly the functions of the Deaconess and Church Sister.

In 1949 the Home Board presented a scheme for the amalgamation of the Order of Deaconesses with the other women working in the Church. Church Sisters would be set apart as Deaconesses by their Presbyteries. Within this new Order of Deaconesses there would be three groups:

* Those working as assistants in parishes: this would include preaching the word, chaplains, teachers of religious instruction in schools or similar spheres of service. (It was however to be some years before Deaconesses would be allowed to preach.)
* Youth, probation and moral welfare work, personnel management, nursing, psychotherapy;
* Other parochial work.

All training was to include a two years training course at St Colm's College, while the Order was to operate under the Women's Home Mission Committee.

The scheme was approved for a period of five years, at which time the Women's Home Mission Committee would present a permanent scheme for approval.

Mary Levison, commenting on this amalgamation of the 'Brown Deaconesses' with the more numerous Church Sisters, stated it had been said that during the twenty years in the United Church:[xv] '*The*

40

Deaconesses had presented the United Church with a perpetual constitutional problem, while the Church Sisters, as employees of Committees, were no problem at all'.

D. P. Thomson, commenting on how long it had taken the Church to approve a united Order of Deaconesses, wrote:[xvi] *'It is this kind of almost endless delay and quibbling which has so handicapped and frustrated what might well have been the most significant modern movement in the Church of Scotland'.*

Margaret Allan DCS remembered the turbulent journey to the merging of the two groups. Writing in the Deaconess Newsletter she said she would never forget sitting in the gallery of the General Assembly hall on an occasion when the Convener of the Order of Deaconesses presented a report recommending that the Order of Deaconesses be abandoned. The Clerk of the Presbytery of Hamilton, however, moved an amendment in support of the Order being retained, talking of the pioneering work done by the Scottish Deaconesses at home and abroad for many years. The amendment carried and discussions continued.

Margaret also remembered the tensions there were between the two groups. When two 'grey' Church Sisters found themselves with two 'brown' Deaconesses at an ecumenical conference on the Place of Women in the Church, they wondered how to do something more together, and suggested they sit at the same table for dinner that evening. In discussion about the way ahead they decided when they went home they would gather 'seven grey' to meet 'seven brown' informally. This led to the request by the Church Sister Association to investigate how to join the two groups with the name Deaconess being kept for all.

Margaret asked *'Was it only history? And yet looking back we see God's Hand in the events of the past years and take courage and understanding and hope for the future'.*

8

Parish Sisters and Church Sisters

'He calleth his own by name ... and they follow him for they know his voice.'
(John 10: 3-4)

Parish Sisters

Mrs Mary McGillivray

Mrs Mary McGillivray, the first President of the Deaconess Council, began work as a Parish Sister. She was widowed while young and with a young family. Her first appointment was to St Bride's Church, Edinburgh in 1925 where she soon got to know every household in the twelve hundred-strong congregation. She was in charge of the Primary Department of the Sunday School and had a Bible Class of eighty made up of both boys and girls, as well as being Guardian of the Girls Guildry Company. She attended the meetings of the Woman's Guild, Mothers' Union and a nursery meeting to which young mothers brought their little children. She served at St Bride's for ten years.

Mary's second call was to work among the fisher-folk, serving medically, socially and spiritually in Lerwick, Shetland, and in Orkney. It involved long hours attending to the women, who often worked until midnight, when they came to get hand-dressings after gutting the herring. At Great Yarmouth and Lowestoft they were thrilled by the singing at the evening services which were so packed that the doors often had to be closed to keep out the overflow congregation.

In 1941, during the war, she took charge of the rest centre in Lowestoft for naval men who came for home-made soup and a square meal. Before long a large rest room and canteen were opened under the auspices of the Huts and Canteens Committee. Sirens, underground shelters and blackouts were all part of their daily routine. One night the bombs fell and the centre was wrecked but none of them were hurt. She also served in a factory in Fraserburgh among girls and women during the war years.

The Home Mission Committee had taken special interest in the welfare of service-women in hospital throughout the war. The work was successful and Mrs McGillivray was appointed to explore the possibilities of also approaching civilians in hospital. At first there was mistrust until she received a letter from Edinburgh Presbytery authorizing her appointment. She began visiting in four hospitals as Assistant Hospital Chaplain. She later took groups to Craigengower, the holiday home at Tighnabruaich, where staff and patients lived together as a family, sharing laughter and fellowship, beauty and peace.

When Mary McGillivray became the first President of the Deaconess Council, she had served the Church as Parish Sister, Church Sister and Deaconess for thirty five years.

Annabella Robertson

In 1927 Miss Robertson went to Deaconess House for a year before being appointed to Charteris Memorial Church as a Parish Sister. The houses the parishioners lived in were small, smoky and dirty. She was adopted as the first Home Missionary of the Girls' Association, which generously provided money for short outings for the children and older folk. It was the time of great unemployment and depression, and one wee boy said '*Ma faither says that Santa Claus is on the 'means test' and canna come to our hoose*'. Thanks to the G.A., Santa overcame the means test.

Moving to Glasgow, Miss Robertson served in Hamilton Hill

Church, the Lodging House Mission and Anderson Old before returning to Edinburgh.

There, Annabella was appointed to Colinton Mains prior to the building of a Church. The congregation worshipped in a hut. The two hundred members of the Primary department of the Sunday School met in the hut while the Beginners' department met in the Deaconess's own home. Miss Robertson's last years of service were spent at St David's Viewforth. She had an active and fulfilled retirement before her death in her 101st year.

Church Sisters

Elizabeth Craig

Elizabeth Craig was described as a pioneer in every sense of the word, with courage to try new ways and a heart big enough to accept failure and try again. After living in Lausanne she trained at St Colm's when it was the United Free Church College, and was appointed as a Church Sister in St John's UF Church in Dundee. She served on the Staff of St Colm's from 1921 to 1924. It was while she was there she had the idea of arranging a holiday for mothers. With a great deal of persuading eight women went with '*the college ladies*' to a church hall in Bonnyrigg where they all felt they were a long way from home - all of six miles! The holidays later progressed from church halls to a seaside villa.

When team work began in the West Fife villages, Elizabeth was given the task, along with Lysbeth Livie, of training probationer Church Sisters who went there straight from college. Other members of the team in West Fife were Dorothy Gardner, Nellie White and Margaret Gardner. When this work ceased, Elizabeth became Church Sister in Govan Parish Church and then at Craigiemains, Dundee. She was to go on be Matron of an Approved School in Edinburgh where she introduced advanced ideas of freedom where doors were left unlocked. In the Old Parish Church in Govan she introduced ideas for a clothing store after visiting the German Deaconess institution at Kaiserswerth, where she discovered they had a large two-storey house for this work. It was while she was at Govan that she and Miss Lawson from the Home Mission Committee visited Craigengower in Tighnabruaich with a view to it being used as a holiday house to which Deaconesses could bring mothers for the summer months. The House was eventually offered to the Home Mission Committee and continued to be used by Deaconesses into the 1990s. Elizabeth Craig was the last warden of Deaconess House in George Square.

Dorothy Gardner

Dorothy Gardner in 1920 made up her mind she wanted to make dairy farming her career. She began training at the College of Agriculture and went on to work at Inverkip where she had a profound spiritual experience. It was while she was out on her cycle early one morning that the Lord spoke to her: '*I want you to give up the work you love and go and train as a Church Sister and work for me in needy places*'. Dorothy reported her first response as: '*No I will not give up the country life I love, so that is that Lord*'. For weeks she didn't listen but in the summer of 1925 she resigned her post and was enrolled as a student at St Colm's.

She had little interest in theology but the Bible and Church History enthralled her and she was greatly affected by her visits to the Poorhouse and the Edinburgh Magdalene Asylum. At the end of term she was worried that she had little to offer but that day she read in Mrs Hermon's *Book of Creative Prayer*: '*What if God has given you the priceless gift of friendship, joy and enthusiasm, why not give these to God and let them with laughter ring down the corridors of your life to bring help to many*'. She made these gifts her offering at the communion – and throughout her life. She served in Lochgelly,

Trinity Saltcoats, Stenhouse, Edinburgh and was with the fisher-lassies in Lowestoft in 1933.

While working in Greenock, Dorothy, with Sisters Jean Lees, Elizabeth Little and May Mackenzie, began to take mothers to Craigengower at Tighnabruaich. They went for four weeks. The Guild supplied jam, marmalade, cake and groceries, while the holiday makers paid one pound each. They sailed for 5/- return.

Dorothy went on to serve at Cairns Memorial, Edinburgh. In 1954 she went to work with the Huts and Canteens Committee doing pastoral work with British forces in Germany and Cyprus. In 1957 she went to Gilmerton Parish, Edinburgh, while from 1960 to 62 she was in Malaysia.

Dorothy became President of Deaconess Council in 1963 and she attended the World Federation of Deaconesses Conference in Berlin. It was there she offered, on behalf of Scotland, to host the World Conference in 1966.

On her retirement from Thornhill, Stirling, in 1964 she said she wanted people to continue to contact her as in her retirement she would have more time for her prayer life. At Council she could always be found going round with her notebook jotting down where people worked and what they were involved in so that she could pray for them. She had a wonderful celebration on 18 November 1988 of 60 years as a Deaconess.

Frances Danskin

Frances Danskin was the eldest of six. In her home in Motherwell her father gathered his family for worship every night and her invalid grandfather always had an open Bible beside him. She was influenced in her vocation when Betty Duncan, a Church Sister, came to her church in Motherwell. Francis went to St Colm's in

1930, and there she made the words of the college motto her own –
*'He calleth his own by name ... and they follow him for they know his
voice'.*

She began work in St George's Parish Church in Edinburgh and it
was in her time there that she became aware that she belonged not
just to the Church of Scotland but to the Church Catholic through the
great hymns and canticles of the Church. At the end of eight years
she was tired and in need of a break. In 1941 she took up the
challenge of war-work with the ATS (Auxiliary Territorial Service):
through the Church of Scotland Huts and Canteens at Glencorse.
After two years she was appointed as Chaplain's Assistant to the
Signal School at Strathpeffer. She later moved to Edinburgh with the
Signal School and then to Devon until the end of the war.

After that a call came to join the staff at St Colm's College. She had
to be approached twice before she was persuaded to accept. She
agreed to go for a year but was to remain for six years during which
time she said her mind was stretched and enriched. Her years at St
Colm's were a voyage of discovery, about God, people and about
herself. Another beginning for her at this time was her first visit to
Iona where she loved the Abbey services with the prayers of
intercessions for the Community and the prayers of healing both
were later to play such a large part in her ministry.

Her next appointment was to St Columba's Pont Street, London,
where she stayed for 12 years. In her time there she met many broken
people and became aware of the suffering of the world and her
inadequacy to meet it as an individual. It was here and through the
Guild of Pastoral Psychology that she discovered what she spoke of
as *'the saving group'*, a group within a congregation to which any
stranger in any kind of distress could come and be accepted and be
given understanding and encouragement. This prepared her for the
step on her vocation which was to take her as a Deaconess to the
Royal Edinburgh Hospital. Writing after five years of work there, she
said how important it had been simply to be where people were:
*'Sitting where they sat, learning from them, communicating without
words until there emerged a sense of belonging'.* Working alongside

other professions enabled her to recognise the value of different ways and techniques to approach to people and problems. She was elected as President of Deaconess Council and it was during this time there was the beginning of talks towards a Diaconate of men and women.

After five years in the hospital, at the age of 63 she took up a part-time ministry in the world of the hard of hearing. She travelled the Borders and East Lothian. She wrote about how much there was to learn in communicating with lips and fingers and of the isolation and loneliness of the hard of hearing.

After her official retirement in 1974 she gave her whole-hearted commitment to the Edinburgh Centre of the Christian Fellowship of Healing at Holy Corner, where she was appointed chairperson. At the Centre they were deeply grateful for her '*wisdom, tact and grace*'. Her vision, of which she had spoken years before, of a Healing Centre open every day, was now realised. A room in the Centre is named 'The Danskin Room'.

Alice Scrimgeour

Alice Scrimgeour in her quiet way influenced many people. She was a well known figure in the east end of Glasgow and admired by Catholics and Protestants alike. Brought up in Doune she was commissioned a Church Sister in 1938. Alice commented in an interview that the status of a Church Sister had not been very good. Some ministers had appreciated the work they did, while others were scathing. She was 'lent' to the Iona Youth Committee where she was employed by the Church as Youth Organiser of Glasgow and Strathclyde, running summer camps on Iona. Although she had been 'lent' she said the Women's Home Mission Committee had not liked Church Sisters changing over to another Committee.

Alice was a visionary and after the war took over Stroove, a house in Skelmorlie. There she brought young people from Germany and Scotland together to talk and live together in peace and reconciliation. It was also a haven for poor families and young people from Glasgow who couldn't afford a holiday. In the kitchen Alice listened to stories of emotionally broken people, with endless patience and cups of tea and coffee. Her pancakes were famous. Young people would tell their stories around the kitchen table. Several generations of ministers were shaped by Alice's kitchen theology. At the beginning of the troubles in Ireland in the 1970s she brought young people from both communities to Stroove. It was very difficult week and Alice's response at the end of their time was to say '*next time the mothers and aunties would come*' and they did.

She was President of the Deaconess Council from 1970 to 1974 and during which time the Diaconate was looking at reform once again. Alice could recall her earlier time on the Committee for Deaconesses when it was under the Home Mission Committee. Her memories of that time were of how they had to stand and wait in the corridor until the point in the meeting when Deaconess business was being discussed when they were invited in for a short time only. At that time within the Church's structure they were five stages away from having their voice heard in the Assembly. When eventually the Diaconate was given a voice in the courts of the Church, Alice could be found faithfully taking her place as a commissioner at Assembly remaining right to the end of late night sessions before getting the train home to Glasgow – by that stage she was in her late eighties. She was a faithful member of Presbytery until 2007.

In 1976 Alice Scrimgeour was nominated for the 'Scotswoman of the Year' award by *The Evening Times*. She was overwhelmed by being given the rosebowl award by Frankie Vaughan.

Margaret Allan

Margaret Allan was influenced by the 1910 Edinburgh World Mission Conference in her early youth. She was appointed a Church Sister in Peterhead in 1937 and was to serve as a 'grey' Church Sister for four years and then was a 'brown' Deaconess for four years before the two came under the care of one Committee. She was on the first executive of the International Federation of Deaconesses formed in 1946 and never lost her vision of the power and inspiration a Deaconess Fellowship could mean on a world scale. Scotland was to continue to play a major role in what became World DIAKONIA.

Margaret enjoyed the emphasis and work of the Iona Community, and shared in it as an Associate Member.

She became one of the leaders in the pioneering work at the Davidson Clinic in 1953 at a time when there was perceived conflict between the insights of the work of psychology and faith. Her life long concern, along with others, led to the formation of the Scottish Pastoral Association. She made a unique contribution to the founding of the Association through her conviction, initiative and drive in the furtherance of its development and understanding in the caring professions. All of this was at a time when her own health was failing. Today the Scottish Association of Pastoral Care and Counselling still hold an annual Margaret Allan Lecture.

In an article in the Deaconess Newsletter entitled '*From a shut in*,' she wrote '*instead of being afflicted, the real truth was that 'shut ins' were receiving a vocation most special and valuable to God'*. Psalm 35 verse 20 speaks of the '*quiet in the land*'. She wrote, '*Let the whole day be linked to the Lord by words of adoration, a cry for help or thanksgiving. In intercessions colleagues, friends, students need our prayers, or someone who brings your meal, or a neighbour when we hear their voice, or the sound of children, the milkman the postman, the people watching the same TV programme as you. Once you begin this game you can find you are going places, adventuring in a new country*'.

Telling of Margaret's death in the Newsletter, Dorothy Gardner wrote that Margaret's prayers surrounded her fellow Deaconesses through all her long years of illness. She was someone who had a sense of fun and saw the rich potentials in the ugly and rejected of human life. The Rev. Ian Ireland said at her funeral that, '*She had a dogged insistence, (at times exasperating) on what she felt was laid upon her heart to uphold*'.

Effie Gray

Effie Gray was set apart as a Church Sister in 1939 although the Assembly report in 1936 advised she was accepted as a candidate for the Diaconate. On 23 January 1950 she was commissioned as a Deaconess at a service in St Giles Cathedral. She served under the Home Mission Committee at King Street, Kilmarnock, and Granton Parish, Edinburgh. From 1946 to 1955, she served as Sunday School Organiser for the Presbytery of Edinburgh and later for the Synod of Lothian and Tweeddale. In 1955 she joined the staff at St Colm's College using her experience in parish and Christian education to train Deaconesses. When she retired in 1971 she took up work again with the Home Board organising Playgroups before returning, 1972, as a Deaconess on a temporary part-time basis at St Martin's Portobello. Effie finally retired in 1975.

Chrissie Denham

Chrissie Denham was set apart as a Church Sister in Aberdeen in 1940 before being appointed to Nigeria with the Overseas Council where she ran courses for leaders of the Guild in the Presbyteries. She also ran refresher courses for Church Sisters and other women workers. In 1967, along with Aku Oku, a Nigerian, Chrissie began a training course at the Goldie Lay Training Centre for women evangelists and a two year course for Church Sisters. They were looking for women with a higher qualification for Church Sister work, this would include women who would become Guild organisers and social workers in the Church. There were plans to create a Nigerian Order of Deaconesses. With the beginning of the Nigerian civil war in 1967 they became more involved in working with refugees and the Red Cross. The Sisters became scattered and many were themselves refugees. Chrissie had eventually to return home.

In 1969 she was appointed to Holy Trinity, Wester Hailes, where she was commissioned as a Deaconess. She was appointed to Richmond Craigmillar Church in 1970 where she was to remain until she retired. When she attended Council in retirement Chrissie could always be found amongst the younger Deaconesses saying that she enjoyed their company rather than that of her contemporaries. Chrissie was always delighted if someone called unexpectedly to take her out, describing it as '*a day of lovely surprises*'.

In 1992 in recognition of her service in the Presbyterian Church in Nigeria's East Synod, the Woman's Guild named a new school for girls at Umuagu after her. The vocational school was for girls of 12 and upwards and taught sewing crafts and vocational skills.

Elspeth Webster

Elspeth Webster had been involved in her home church in Burntisland in her youth. She intended to do teacher training but her mother died and she felt she was needed at home. At one point she wrote to ask about employment at the orphanage at Bridge of Weir, but her minister went to see her father and told him about Church Sisters. She was interviewed by Chris Lawson (the Home Mission Secretary), Miss Moinet (the Principal of St Colm's), and Dr Mary Dodds – and was accepted to train as a Church Sister. Her father had to pay for her training at St Colm's.

On arrival, a second year student showed her round the College. After dinner on the first evening they were given a lecture on how to keep books. Rules were strict in the first year. They had to be careful about dress, and had to dress for dinner in the evening. A member of staff sat at the table and students had to learn to circulate. As well as Biblical Studies there were lectures on Church History and Pastoral work. A kindergarten was run in the College; House Guilds were held; there was practical work – visits in Stockbridge and the Pleasance, on which they had to give a report on their return to college.

When preparing an address for the Mothers' Meeting students would go across to the Botanic Gardens and rehearse their speech. Miss Moinet would be present when they gave their talk and would give a crit on it afterwards. Students had to be ready and able to turn their hand to anything: Guildry, Guides, clubs for girls. Evenings were for study if they were not out on practical work, and Miss Moinet would wander the corridors to make sure students were working. At the end of first year Elspeth went on a summer placement to Swanwick. Before she went she was giving a lecture by Miss Moinet about not being shy and making sure she spoke out. Miss Nicol was Principal in her second year when there was a lighter atmosphere in college.

Miss Lucy Brown Douglas, one of the Presbyterial Council Committee members, invited St Colm's students for lunch on Saturdays and afterwards they were taken for a drive or played an Indian board-game called Parcheesi before being driven back to the college by the chauffeur. Open House was held in College on a Friday afternoon, when people could come for afternoon tea.

When the war broke out in 1939 the students had to cut up thick cardboard to make blackouts and the chapel at St Colm's was used as the air raid shelter.

At the end of training, Elspeth was sent to Aberdeen where she was interviewed by the minister and Session Clerk. She did a six month probationary period before being set apart as a Church Sister on 31 March 1941. There she was working in the downtown areas of the city, where people were poor and TB was prevalent. She had to attend the prayer meeting before the Sunday service. She was involved with Mothers' Meetings which were usually meetings for the older women. The women who attended these meetings did not consider themselves well dressed enough to go to a morning service. Guilds provided produce through the Home Mission Committee and the Church Sisters would collect it to be distributed. The Church Hall was taken over as a rest centre during the war where people sheltered from bombs. There were two nights when they had raids and the Hall was packed: the minister looked in briefly but left Elspeth to organise things.

She was appointed to St George's Parish Church in Edinburgh in 1943, a congregation of contrast between the very wealthy and the poor. She worked amongst the poor, visiting houses where generations of families lived together in one house and if a relative died, the coffin was kept in the house with the children playing round about. In spite of the poverty pennies and halfpennies would be brought for the work of Foreign Mission.

She was appointed to Gilmerton in 1952. She later served in Dundee, Grangemouth, and finally Rosyth. Her work was restricted to working with women and girls. However there was one occasion, when a group of boys asked why they couldn't come to the Bible Class; Elspeth mentioned this to her minister and that was the beginning of a (mixed) Youth Fellowship.

The work in these Church Extension parishes was mainly in the huge Sunday Schools, visiting and attending women's meetings. The Church Sister or Deaconess had just to do as she was told in the parishes and they were given their visiting list by the minister.

It was during Elspeth's time at St George's that she was recognised as a Deaconess at a service in St Giles Cathedral on 23 January 1950 after the General Assembly of 1949 had decreed that the Church Sisters and Deaconesses would become one order of Deaconesses. Being herself a Church Sister, she had not had much to do, in the early days, with the Deaconesses. The Sisters never saw the 'Brown

Deaconesses'. Her impression was that many of them were ladies doing charitable work.

Elspeth was President of the Church Sisters at the time when proposals were being brought about changes in the Scheme to the Office of Deaconess. The last meeting of the Church Sisters was held in St George's Church in Charlotte Square in Edinburgh, now West Register House. Elspeth was President. When the new Deaconess Council was formed, it was Elspeth who pinned the Badge on the President Mrs McGillivray. Elspeth remembers being asked to model the new grey uniform which was then introduced. They were given a costume: two skirts, two blouses, a coat and hat. The dress had a cross-over bodice with a high neck which they could put linen round, a bit like a collar. Uniforms had to last three years, and were made by Wilkies.

Their uniform was worn most of the time. She remembered being invited to a dance which Princess Elizabeth (the present Queen) and Prince Phillip attended, soon after their engagement. Princess Elizabeth was resplendent in a powder blue dress, while Elspeth went to the dance in a dress borrowed from her landlady. They went to the Garden Party every year, in uniform. Deaconesses were not well paid. Salary was £100 per year then it went up to £120. They had to find their own digs to stay in and were at the mercy of the landlady, who could ask them to move if she had family or friends coming. They were under The Women's Home Mission Committee and at each post, the local Presbyterial Council Home Mission Committee would take an interest in them and invite them for a meal.

Mary Rhind

Mary was born in Aberdeen on 26 August 1918. After graduating MA and BSc in 1941 from the University of Aberdeen, Mary offered herself for service with the Church and went to St Colm's for training.

She served first in St Bride's, Partick, and long before youth camps existed on Iona, she was taking campers to the North End where they learned that Iona far from being a quiet escape was the launching pad for service on the mainland. It was after finishing at St Bride's that Mary was set apart on 14 May 1944 as a Church Sister. She served at Pittodrie and Northfield in Aberdeen, where there were 1600 in the Sunday School and 400 in the Bible class. She arranged training classes for 200 teachers and youth workers.

After a time at St James, Pollock, the Home Board appointed Mary as the Church of Scotland's team member with the Danesholme Ecumenical Experiment in Corby where she was to serve for seventeen years. The motto of the town of Corby is 'Deeds not words'. Mary described it as a town of change, movement and opportunity. People came from Scotland, Ireland, Wales or Latvia. In this new and bustling, exciting situation the Church faced problems in a critical way. Mary was a member of the Ecumenical Church in Danesholme. Through the various groups they got to know each other. There was a group to plan worship, one for contemplative prayer and another 'who cares for the carers'. Neighbourhood services were held from time to time, when people in the community shared their concerns and supported each other in prayer: the schools, the clinic, the district councillors, etc.

All the old concepts were being questioned and they were prepared to alter structures to meet the rapidly changing needs of the town, where there were equal numbers of Catholics and Scottish Presbyterians. The other half of the 45,000 population were mainly Anglican, Congregational, Methodist, Baptist, Lutheran/Latvian,

6. Fiona Gordon, Connie Philip, Kay Ramsey

7. Elspeth Webster and Mrs McGillivray First President Deaconess Council

9. Norma Ronald

8. Elma Sloan

58

10. Annabella Robertson's 100th Birthday

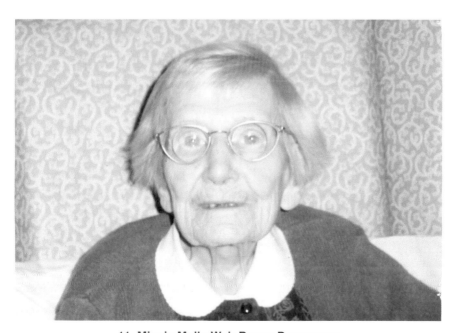

11. Minnie Mullo Weir Brown Deaconess

12. Ellen Rutherford Strathconon

13. Stella Reekie

14. Sheena Mc Naughton Play group Adviser

15. Maureen Hutchison First Married Deaconess

61

16. Morag Crawford - Nursery

17. Morag Crawford Work place Chaplaincy.

18. Helen Hughes Asylum Seekers

19. Ann Lyall Lodging House Mission

20. Mark Evans

21. Planning Group 1966 Conference

22. Kay Ramsay SEED Conference

65

23. DRAE Conference, Stirling

24. Conference Stirling, 1994

25. African Delegates DRAE Conference

26. DRAE Presidents

28. Guild Diaconate and Life and Work represented 125 Anniversary

29. Morag Crawford and former students

30. Pat Munro President 2013-

31. Early Deaconess Badge

32. Order of Deaconess badge

33. President's Badge

34. Deacon Badge Mid 1990s- present time

35 Church Sister Badge

72

Serbian and Salvation Army: the church was fragmented by its many denominations. However this led to (a) a programme of ecumenical evangelism for the town; (b) planning towards an ecumenical parish experiment in the Danesholme area of South Corby; (c) the hope was to set up a single Christian Congregation – reaching out to people moving into the area. In order to do this people had to be prepared to lay aside their strongly held convictions and accept each other. They needed the freedom to experiment and take risks and be allowed to make mistakes. They needed pioneers, seeking to work through issues that arose through their actions relating to social responsibilities, Christian Aid, house groups and special interest groups and visiting.

In time Mary was employed by the Corby Council of Churches, and not by the Home Board. Funding came from the Corby Development Corporation, The Corby Urban Council and The Northants Council. She continued to develop pioneering work liaising between the statutory bodies and volunteers from all the churches under the auspices of the Social Responsibility Committee of the Council of Churches. She was given the name Community Liaison Officer and in this capacity engaged with, encouraged and supported people working in voluntary work in Corby, discovering which needs were not being met.

In November 1979 the end of iron and steel making in Corby was formally announced and the town faced major unemployment, having been founded around one major industry. Mary was one of the representatives on the Youth Opportunity Programme. The programme tried to ensure the young people would have some opportunity for training under supervision. Other initiatives included an organiser appointed for children 'at risk,' a Friends and Family Service was set up, also a telephone service for parents in a crisis situation who were tempted to harm their children.

In 1981 Mary retired and returned to Scotland, working on a special project with the Iona Community in relation to unemployment. She joined the Iona Community in 1982. She believed passionately and worked vigorously for the cause of Nuclear Disarmament, being a member of the Gareloch Horticulturalists who raise their signs and bear witness around the Gareloch against Trident and Polaris.

Mary loved climbing the mountains in Scotland. Her last holiday was with a group of retired Deaconesses to the Spean Bridge area. One afternoon they had a trip on the ski lift up Aonach Mor. I remember her recollecting the wonderful view they had had. Her face shone, she had been to the mountain top in more ways than one. A few weeks later she was admitted to hospital where she died supported at the end by her Diaconate Family, the family of the Iona Community and the 'Gareloch Hortis'.

Betty White

Betty White grew up in Rutherglen. During World War II she worked as an inspector of a small tools factory in Lanarkshire. After the war she went to St Colm's to train as a Church Sister. Her first placement was to Burntisland, and she was commissioned as a Deaconess in St Columba's Church in 1950.

In 1951 Betty moved to Glasgow, Cardonald until 1958. She served successively in St Andrew's, Irvine; Castlemilk East Church; The Gorbals; Rutherglen Road, Polmadie. In 1977 she went on to do further study, taking a course in Pastoral Studies at Trinity College, Glasgow. This was followed by three years at St Paul's, Provanmill. Betty's last place of service was in Royston at Townhead, Blochairn where she also worked beyond retirement and even for a time with no pay. It was there she was licensed to preach.

When she first went to Royston there was no roof on the church hall. Betty was concerned that the young people had no place to go. There was no money available from Church resources so Betty sought the help of Sir Malcolm Rifkind, the then Scottish Secretary and eventually the church hall was restored.

Betty's enthusiasm instigated the beginning of youth clubs, a 'nearly-new shop', and a meeting place for older members but her main achievement was the Rainbow Club for young people. Betty had a real heart for the young people and worked tirelessly for them, even supporting them when they went to court. She took them away to centres like Iona, Stroove, Carberry and the Badenoch Centre, and the Centre never forgot Betty and her young people!

Betty was President of Council from 1977 -80 thus becoming the first President of the new Diaconate Council in 1979. She was influential in bringing in the introduction of the Diaconate of men and women. In 1978 she introduced a male German Deacon, Lothar Schulz, to Council and he highlighted the Diaconate as a ministry of outreach into the life of the world, responding as Christ did to the needs of the people. He presented the role of the Diaconate as that of 'enabler' to the congregation of God's people to fulfil their mission and service in the world. He told how Deacons in Germany were trained in a particular skill as well as a theological qualification. He saw the ministry not as an individualistic one but to 'spark community'. He saw the Diaconal dimension of the Church as not only to help people in need but also to intervene in an unjust society. Betty and Council were inspired by his challenges and certainly later she would bring proposals on social issues to Council through the Glasgow Diaconal group.

Betty White was dedicated to the Diaconate and to the wider Church. Some words used at her funeral sum up Betty: '*elegant, remarkable, dedicated and faithful*'.[xvii]

9

After the Second World War: the 1950s and 1960s

'Get ready and go south .... Do you understand what you are reading?'
(Acts 8: 26f)

The parish work of Deaconesses, Parish Sisters and Church Sisters from the early years to the Second War had mainly been in downtown areas where there was much overcrowding and poverty with resulting poor health and inability to pay for medical care necessitating the need for the nursing element in the early training. The work had mainly been amongst the women and children. Now the post-war years had brought about changes in society with the introduction of a National Health Service and welfare state benefits. So the report of the Home Board in 1951 stated that the Church '... *must be continually pioneering and seeking out new avenues of service. The Order of Deaconesses being an integral part of the Church's life is subject to the same necessity, if it is to remain vital throughout years of change'.*

New housing developments were taking place and people were moving out from the downtown areas to the vast new housing estates, away from family and friends and all that was familiar. There were few shops or facilities; there was a feeling of isolation and insecurity. The work of Church Extension grew rapidly as new churches and halls were built and new congregations formed. In the new housing areas the work of Deaconesses involved door to door visiting, making contact with the people new to the area inviting them to the church. Family support which had been readily available in the past was no longer there. There was instability of the world in which the young people were growing up. By the mid fifties there was an increase in employment of married women and this was reflected in the dropping attendance at the women's meetings. Help was needed for young mothers; there was a lack of leaders for youth activities. There was a change of emphasis on the work and opportunities to work out imaginative new techniques for mission.

In 1951 there were six students in training at St Colm's as well as two graduates at University. But by 1954 there was a downward trend and the intake was not enough to cover the loss of the current number of Deaconesses; by 1955 the employing Committee was unable to meet new requests for Deaconesses. How was the Diaconal ministry to develop to meet the needs of the time?

It had been hoped the coming together of the Deaconesses and Church Sisters would bring in a settled period. Instead it brought in a period of questioning by different groups on what an 'Order' meant for the Church of Scotland and what the special function of a Deaconess was, as well as about their relationship to the Courts of the Church; and also about the dual role of the Home Board as an employing and care committee. A new Commission was appointed, which recognised that from the time of the Union of the Churches any attempt to redefine the Order had always been on a temporary basis and '*was superseded before it had been properly gripped by the church*'.[xviii] There was, however, no representation of Deaconesses on the Commission, giving the Deaconesses the feeling that the issues had not been adequately addressed. When invited to comment on a draft report, they argued that Dr Charteris had intended the office of Deaconess to be an order of ministry in the Church and not a voluntary membership of an association, group or sisterhood. They also raised the issue of the Deaconess being the servant of the whole Church and not merely constituting a section of it. Further, an office of ministry surely meant eligibility to sit in the courts of the Church.

Following the Commission's report in 1948, there were some positive moves forward. A Deaconess Council was set up, giving the Deaconesses an opportunity to discuss their own affairs and to voice their collective opinions on the wider work in the Church. The Committee on the Order of Deaconesses became one of the Standing

Committees of the General Assembly, reporting directly to the Assembly rather than through the Home Board, and the Committee was to be allowed to approach the Church for funds for the administration of its work. Salaries and pensions of Deaconesses were paid by the employing Committees. Moreover five Deaconesses would represent the Order on the new Committee. It was also agreed that Deaconesses with the necessary qualifications should be licensed to preach, and Mary Lusk (Levison) was the first to be so licensed on 20 January 1957. Parochial Deaconesses were given the right to attend Kirk Session meetings when aspects of their work was being discussed and they were to be represented on appropriate Committees of Presbytery and General Assembly.

The first Deaconess Council took place 11-12 June 1957 in the Martin Hall at New College. The first President was Mrs Mary McGillivray DCS, and the Council was described as a '*little General Assembly of Deaconesses*' by the Committee's Convener, the Rev. Roy Sanderson. The then Moderator of the General Assembly, the Rt. Rev. George MacLeod, visited the Council, thus setting the pattern for future years of the Moderator or other representative bringing greetings from the General Assembly. Elspeth Webster the retiring President of the Association presented the new President's badge to Mrs McGillivray. The badge had been modelled on the Celtic design of the normal Deaconess badge but it had a Presbyterian blue background. The Council encouraged the setting up of local Associations where Deaconesses could discuss policy issues as well as receiving spiritual support and fellowship. A Newsletter was introduced and a prayer guide to help Deaconesses in their private intercessions. By the end of the fifties in order to make a link between the employing committee and the Deaconesses more personal, each member of the Women's Home Mission Committee had been linked with a small group of Deaconesses to get to know them individually and a day Conference was held twice a year.

The major work of the early sixties was the continued development of work in the new housing estates; however a few Deaconesses were also appointed in rural areas. In the downtown areas although the older folk were better off with free medical care and pensions, many were lonelier than before as families had moved out to the new housing areas and there was demolition going on around them. Deaconesses were involved in setting up Circles of Friendship for men and women.

In the new housing areas the young marrieds were amongst strangers with no shops or cinemas, many had no experience of budgeting. Too often it seemed that children were sent to Sunday School to get them out of the way. Deaconesses were reporting hundreds – sometimes a thousand children in Sunday Schools, with a consequent need for training leaders and teachers. Summer church schools were started; opportunities developed to go into primary and secondary schools. Bible study groups and house groups were springing up; modern translations of the Bible were being used; adult education was increasing as more adults were drawn in through their children coming to Sunday School. Contacts were made with other social agencies. By the mid 1960s play groups were being set up in church halls. Links were made with the Guild's Presbyterial Councils through the 'adoption' scheme of a Deaconess who would go to the Council two or three time a year to speak about her work. The Woman's Guild branches would support her work in various ways often through gifts of food and clothing which were distributed to the needy. It was hoped the links would develop into two way links between the congregations.

In response to these social changes, in 1962 training for Deaconesses was adjusted to include a one year course in Social Studies at Glasgow University as well as the two years at St Colm's.
In 1961 the Committee on the Order of Deaconesses had presented another draft scheme to the Assembly, which was considered by Presbyteries and Committees and adopted by the Assembly the following year. Emphasis was placed on the office of ministry rather than the Order. 'The Committee was renamed 'The Deaconess Board'. During the consultations, one Presbytery suggested that ten years would be an appropriate time to review the new proposals to give time to settle. Although other schemes were introduced they were not passed and when the Diaconate was opened to men and women, minor amendments were made to the 1962 scheme. Much of

the present Act is based on the 1961/2 Scheme as revised to include the additional changes the years brought. The new Board was intended to have the welfare of Deaconesses as its primary concern, and this was probably the period when they enjoyed the greatest autonomy, being a Board of the General Assembly. A new, coordinated way of raising funds for the whole Church also removed the necessity of the women of the church to raise money exclusively for Diaconal salaries and pensions.

The 1960s was the time when there was probably the greatest variety of service for the Deaconesses. In 1965, of the 70 active Deaconesses, 46 were employed by the Women's Home Mission Committee in parishes or in hospital chaplaincy; seven served on the Committee of Religious instruction for Youth as Sunday School Organisers or Organisers of Senior Youth, two were with the Social and Moral Welfare Board; two with the Ladies Highland Association and two on the Staff of St Colm's College. There was one serving with the Huts and Canteens Committee; one with the headquarters staff of the Overseas Council and one with the Joint Committee for Overseas Students. There were five Deaconesses not in the employment of the Church of Scotland: one was probation officer; one a National Children's Society officer; one with Scottish Sunday School Union; one with the National Bible Society of Scotland; and one was undergoing training to qualify her to work with handicapped children.

Continuing consideration of the Diaconate was to become part of the wider debate as the whole question of the place of women in the Church was raised. Mary Lusk DCS (Levison) petitioned the General Assembly in 1963 for admittance to the Ministry of Word and Sacrament. Her story is told in her book *'Wrestling with the Church.'* In 1966 legislation was changed to allow women to be ordained as elders and two years later, in 1968, the Ministry of Word and Sacrament was opened to women. The first woman to be ordained was a Deaconess, the Rev. Catherine McConnachie. It was to be ten years later, in 1978, before Mary Levison herself was ordained to the Ministry of Word and Sacrament. Mary had married

Fred Levison in 1965. In 1974 Mary was elected President of Deaconess Council for three years.

Meanwhile lots of questions were being asked in regard to the Diaconate. Was there was still a need for a Diaconate in the Church? The World Conference held in Edinburgh in 1966 had convinced the Deaconesses there was still a need for a serving ministry. The Church of Scotland Panel on Doctrine raised questions about ordination for Deaconesses although the Deaconesses themselves were split on the issue. In 1967 the Deaconess Board raised the possibility of Deaconesses being members of the courts of the Church; however questions were raised as to what would then happen in regard to other categories of worker. Rev. David Doig, Convener of the Home Board, raised the question of one Diaconate of men and women.

The next decade was to be a time when not only the Church of Scotland but all the major denominations were looking at the office of the Diaconate in the Church. In the world Church, diaconia was developing to include men as well as women.

By the end of the 1960s increasing recruitment to the Diaconate in Scotland was urgent. There was more team-working in the parishes, sometimes involving a minister with a Deaconess and Lay Missionary or assistant minister. In 1968 the Home Board held a joint conference for Deaconesses and Lay Missionaries. There was greater involvement for Deaconesses in worship and leading services, while in rural areas Deaconesses were helping with pulpit supply, and some were beginning to conduct funerals. Deaconesses were now being involved in baptismal visits to families – as had been suggested back in the forties. New methods were being introduced in Sunday School; some Deaconesses were invited to serve on Congregational Boards. There was certainly an increased understanding in the Church of the potential for Diaconal ministry.

10

Years of Struggle: to the present day Diaconate

'Then a man came and wrestled with him until just before daybreak.
... You have struggled with God and with men and you have won.'
(Genesis 32: 24a, 28b)

At the beginning of the 1970s the Home Board report said that the
work schedules for Deaconesses revealed the vital role they played in
congregations and communities. It also said that every congregation
that had a Deaconess had its life enriched and its outlook broadened
by the gifts, training and dedicated service a Deaconess gave.
Deaconesses at this time were often allocated rentals of Council
houses and were the only professional, caring person living in largely
working class parishes. In the early 70s the reports of the Home
Board were saying that demand for Deaconesses was not abating and
there was a need for more students. They stressed the need for a
trained, commissioned, mobile Diaconate ready to meet the needs of
Church, parish and community wherever the need arose. By the mid-
70s they were expressing regret that numbers employed were
diminishing and that because of financial restraints recruitment had
fallen. Payment at this time was 70% of the minimum stipend for
ministers, and without the provision of a house that the parish manse
offered to ministers.

The recruitment age for Deaconesses was lowered to eighteen.
Training at St Colm's changed to include, as well as their term time
attachments to parishes, two one-week practical work assignments
which would give them a greater variety of experience. They also did
two-year further training in Pastoral Studies at the universities of St
Andrew's, Glasgow, or Edinburgh; or Christian Education at
Edinburgh University or a placement with the Social Work
Department or a certificate in Youth and Community work. Training
for mature students varied according to age and experience.

During the 1970s a series of proposals and consultations to reform (again) the Diaconate moved between the Boards, the General Assembly and the Presbyteries of the Church. A joint group was set up between the Home Board and the Deaconess Board (and including representation from the Lay Missionaries and the Deaconesses) to look at a renewed Diaconate in the Church, which would be integrated as part of the whole ministry of the Church. A distinctive ministry was sought, to be complementary to the Ministry of Word and Sacrament. The reformed Diaconate would be thought of in terms of service to the world and its needs; to offer training and to encourage the laity in their ministries of service; and to enable the Church to fulfil her ministry of diaconia to the world. Such Deacons would be fully integrated as officeholders and servants of the whole Church, not merely of the Women's section or of one Committee.

As discussion developed, the main proposals were:
* A Diaconate of men and women – with the term 'Deacon' being used.
* Deacons could serve in a variety of positions –
    a) in a congregation or special grouping; or in a congregation where there was no ordained minister;
    b) in organisations or institutions, e.g. hospitals, prisons, social work etc;
    c) or be commissioned to an new area of work, where society was failing to meet the needs and thus to awaken the conscience of the whole Church to diaconia.
* The Diaconate would take its place in the Courts of the Church.
* The position of Deacon within a team ministry would be one of colleague, not that of minister and assistant. The ministries would be regarded as complementary and mutually dependent with different spheres of responsibility.

The General Assembly welcomed these proposals and in 1974 a detailed scheme was sent for consultation to Presbyteries, with emphasis on:
* Ordination;
* Authority to lead Worship without the need for Licensing;

* Membership of the Courts of the Church;
* A Council of the Diaconate;
* Associate Deacons who would not necessarily commit themselves for life.

The responses from Presbyteries were mixed. When it came back to the General Assembly the scheme was not approved, one Commissioner described the Diaconate as '*an untidy anomaly in the Church*'. There had been a profound misunderstanding of the scheme.

There remained an urgent need in the most needy parishes in the land for the work carried out by Deaconesses and Lay Missionaries, yet the Home Board over the next few years highlighted falling numbers of staff, difficulties in meeting budgets. The Church needed to be fully informed to raise finance for training and recruitment.

The Diaconate were encouraged in their thinking by an address given at Diaconate Council in 1976 by Professor T. F. Torrance when he stated the Deacons in the early Church were part of the clergy supported by the Church. He said:[xix] '*Athanasius spoke of ministry as from God to Man and man to God. These were complementary. The first represents the presbyterial office. The second, the ministry of man to God is the ministry of response to that Word and represents the Diaconal office. The presbyterial ministry is not completed without the Diaconal ministry. It is the function of that Diaconal agent to get alongside the believer and help him with his response to Word and Sacraments. The Deacon leads the people in their response of praise and prayer.... The Diaconal ministry extends the life of our Lord in caring for the poor and needy. It seeks the response to help people in their worship so that they are lifted up – this is sacramental, it is essentially missionary, it is evangelical*'.

Of Lay Missionaries, Deaconesses and elders, Torrance said that all were Diaconal. He believed both presbyterial and Diaconal offices should be open to both men and women. He also said it was nonsense to restrict the courts of the Church to ministers and elders and saw that: '*When the Diaconate was revived the presbyterate would have to change. When the presbyterate had a real complement*

in the Diaconate then it would see its own office much more clearly.
A Minister has to fulfil his office in a Diaconal way and a Deacon
has to fulfil his response in an authorised way'.

The seventies was a time of struggle, too, in the Methodist Church.
The doors there had opened to accept women into the Ministry of
Word and Sacrament; a number of Methodist Deaconesses became
Presbyters. In 1978 the Division of Ministries recommended that
recruitment cease for Deaconesses. It was a painful time for the
Methodist Order and much hard thinking was done before
Conference resolved in 1986 that the Diaconal Order be opened to
men and women and that they would be ordained to the Diaconate.

Back in Scotland, the seventies saw married women being accepted
for training, although it was to be into the eighties before women
were given maternity leave. Prior to that they had to resign their
position on marriage. Further ahead, in the nineties we had our first
couple who were Deacons: Karen and Jim Hamilton met at St
Colm's and were married in 1993. We have also had a Father and
Son who were Deacons: John Cathcart, and a few years later Paul,
his son, the current Vice President of Council.

In 1979 after its own years of struggle, the Church of Scotland
Deaconess Board asked the General Assembly simply to rename the
approved 1962 scheme the 'Diaconate Scheme', operating with a
Diaconate Board and a Diaconate Council; and to open the office of
the Diaconate to men and women. This was approved. Though the
far-reaching 1974 proposals had been rejected, men with suitable
qualifications and a vocation could now apply to be recognised as
Deacons: the existing Lay Missionaries, meanwhile, remained in
their separate office.

Not approved, however, were the visionary schemes brought to the
Church during this decade by the Committee of Forty [1971 to
1978], which envisaged collaborative ministry and team work within
Scotland's towns. At a time when mission was needed, the Church
was faced with a time of financial restraints; and numbers involved
in mission were being cut. Discussions were going on about the

viability of St Colm's College, but the Committee of Forty's report saw the type of training and education given by St Colm's as being invaluable to their plans, and the Diaconate as being well equipped to be involved in collaborative ministry. I was a student in St Colm's at this time and we were fired up to work collaboratively, to be part of the visionary thinking in the Church. Now almost forty years later we still await Presbyteries to embrace this vision in their planning.

The 1980s saw the impact of further financial pressures. The number of Deacons employed by the Home Board fell to 61. At the end of 80s there was a rationalisation of the Boards and Committees of the General Assembly, with the Diaconate Board being reduced to a Committee reporting under the Board of Ministry and Mission. Deaconesses could now be invited to be Corresponding [ie non–voting] members of Presbytery. The Church's attitudes to the Diaconate were still ambivalent, as the 1987 report of the Diaconate Committee said:[xx] '*The Diaconate does not fit comfortably into either the thinking or the structures of the Presbyterian Church. Deaconesses are enablers whose function is often to stir up congregations in their response to the Ministry of Word and Sacrament, and the Diaconate as a whole appears still to represent to the Church an unfamiliar, an awkward, a not yet fully accepted form of ministry. Even now on the eve of the centenary in 1988 of Deaconess service, the Church still seems uncertain what to do with these skilled and willing servants – how to integrate them, how to care for them*'. It cannot have helped that since the 1970s the Home Board, acting as the employing agency, had changed their term of reference (or job description) for Deaconesses working in parishes from 'Deaconess' to 'Lay Workers', a term which also included their Lay Missionaries.

Lady Grisell Baillie having been set apart as the first Deaconess on 9 December 1888, 1988 was the Centenary year of Deaconesses in the Church of Scotland. After so many years of struggle, events took a surprising leap forward that year, when the Lay Missionaries resolved to seek recognition and admission to the office of Deacon. Seventeen (all but two) were admitted as Deacons at a service in Renfield St. Stephen's Church, Glasgow, 9 June 1988.

Another positive step was a deliverance received in 1987 from the floor of the Assembly to instruct the Panel on Doctrine to consider the ministry of Diaconate and its relationship to the courts of the Church. In 1989 the Panel reported, saying Deacons were full-time salaried servants of the Church who were a mobile task force capable of providing ministry at the points of greatest need in parishes and in wider spheres of service:[xxi] *'They were trained to teach and equip others, to lead and train leaders so that they might move on to another task – there will always be a place for such a distinctive ministry of encouraging the ministry of the whole people of God'.* The Panel also said Deacons should have a place in the courts of the Church as they were authorised to fulfil specific tasks and were at the disposal of the Church. Finally, proposals to recognise the Diaconate as a component of the Church equal in status to the Eldership and the Ministry of Word and Sacrament went through the Assembly of 1991. The case was well presented by Rev. James Weatherhead, then Principal Clerk, and the legislation went through without opposition. It was a fitting end for Rev. Mary Levison's time as Convener of the Diaconate Committee, as she had seen and been involved in so many struggles for the Diaconate over the years. Deacons were thus accepted and welcomed into the courts of the Church. Very soon, in acknowledgment of their service, Presbyteries began to elect Deacons as their Moderators. Today the wisdom and service available within the Diaconate is further recognised by the many practical responsibilities that individual Deacons exercise within their Presbyteries.

Unchanging from the beginning of the Diaconate in the 19th century, though, was the separation between those recognising and ordering the Diaconate within the Church, and those who appointed and employed individual Deacons. Back in the 1890s, while the Committee on Christian Life and Work pursued their vision for Deaconesses, the Home Mission Committee separately sought to recruit Parish Sisters. By the 1990s, although the Diaconate as such had achieved a fuller recognition as an integral part of the Church of Scotland, the individual Deacons (the former Deaconesses and Lay Missionaries) were in the main employed by the Board of National Mission who now chose to describe them, not as Deacons, Lay

Missionaries or 'Lay Workers', but as 'Parish Assistants'. Moreover committee structures changed at the Assembly of 1989, which meant the Diaconate Committee came under the Board of Ministry and ceased to report directly to the General Assembly. Rev. Mary Levison, Convener of the Diaconate Committee at the time, argued that being part of ministry was the place where the Diaconate should be. It has to be said the Boards were not all of the same opinion. So began the next period of struggle.

The 1990s was a further time of restructuring within the Church; and the '90s were a period when we swung between highs and lows. The Assembly Council, at the end of the '80s, had been asking questions as to what kind of ministry would be needed for the Church, and it also sought to estimate how many ministers and paid agents the Church could support. To begin with, the Council said there should be an increase in recruitment of up to six staff a year employed by the Board of National Mission, thus encouraging an expansion of the Diaconate. In 1994, however, the Council had second thoughts about its strategic plan and budgets were cut. National Mission put a moratorium on the recruitment of Parish Assistants; Diaconal students already in training were told that no posts would be available for them when they qualified. The decision had the knock–on effect of stopping the recruitment of Deacons. As President of Diaconate Council, I and others had to convince the General Assembly to alter the budget to allow at least the existing students to be employed. Our proposals were approved, but the whole crisis – and especially the moratorium on recruitment – was a blow to the Diaconate, particularly in a year when we were hosting in Scotland the inaugural Conference of the DIAKONIA Africa Europe Region.

The following year, 1995, I became Convener of the Diaconate Committee, the first Deaconess to hold the position, as until we were members of the courts of the Church we could not convene an Assembly Committee. As such I was on the Executive of the Board of Ministry, the only woman on the Executive and the only person who was not a minister. It was not an easy time, being the sole female voice on an all male committee, and also not being a minister. The Board was questioning the role of the Diaconate. Once again there was a lack of understanding about Deacons and what they did. The one encouragement through all of this time was a study undertaken ecumenically which produced the *Windsor Statement on the Diaconate*, reminding the Church that:[xxii] '*Deacons are continually aware of God's call for the Church to be Christ the servant in the world, and focus the servant ministry of the whole Church*'.

By now, though it was agreed that the name 'Deacon' be used collectively of men and women, Deacons were employed by a number of the General Assembly's Committees under a number of job titles. The Board of National Mission still held that those they employed should be known as 'Parish Assistants' or 'Project Workers' (depending on the post). This was a diminishing of the identity of the Deacons, the vast majority of whom were employed by National Mission. Neither did that Board confine its recruitment to parish posts to those recognised as Deacons: the former separation between Deaconesses and Parish Sisters had been replaced by that between Deacons and Project Workers.

In 1997 an instruction, originating from the floor of the Assembly, brought the Panel on Doctrine to consider the ordination of Deacons. At the first meeting I attended, a comment was made by a minister that the Diaconate seemed to be in an awful rush to be ordained! It was only 110 years since Charteris had first put the proposal before the Church! In 2001 the General Assembly agreed that Deacons should be ordained – even although someone on the floor of the Assembly had suggested the report be sent back yet again for further consideration. It took another year for final legislation to be approved, and in addition the Diaconate Scheme was at last put into an Act of Assembly for the first time. Special services were held by Presbyteries so that each Deacon could be individually ordained. In 2001 the Board of Ministry also presented the report '*Deacons of the Gospel*' highlighting Jesus, the one who serves, as the model of the ministry of the Deacon.

The Diaconate as a body had thus been recognised as an integral element of the courts of the Church of Scotland, and the majority of active Deacons had been ordained. Diaconal service was recognised in the structures of the Church as a ministry, as Mary Levison and Dr Charteris had wished. When, therefore, there was a restructuring of the Board of Ministry (which now incorporated the previously separate Committee on Education for the Ministry), the Diaconate Committee had the choice of continuing on its own or becoming integrated within the new Board it seemed right at the time to be integrated within the Ministries Council, although with only 70 Deacons and 1,200 ministers the question was whether the minority voice could still be heard? The Diaconate Committee ceased to be in 1997. There were also discussions as to whether there was any need of a Diaconate Council; but it was recognised, after representatives of the Board of Ministry attended the Windsor Conference, that it is through Diaconate Council we maintain our link with the wider Diakonia of the Church.

Another positive came in 2006 when the Diaconate were recognised as a group who could legally conduct weddings in Scotland. This brought another link with the community as very often the weddings we conduct are for people who have no formal contact with the Church yet wish to have a religious ceremony. Many such requests spring from contact with the Deacon in the community.

Through the Ministries Council, Deacons are now recruited and selected in the same way as other ministries in the Church. Training is the same as the training for Ministers of Word and Sacrament. For a number of years suggestions for a detailed review of training have always been deferred to a later time. Recruitment to the Diaconate is small in the Church of Scotland, though we are encouraged that recruitment in the Methodist Church is increasing. We hope the tide will turn for Deacons in our Church too. There is a need for a ministry in the Church which is flexible, adaptable, works collaboratively and enables others to fulfil their Diaconal service in the world. Today we need a ministry which is able to pioneer new forms of ministry and outreach to the community. The Deacon, following the serving ministry of Jesus the servant, is well able to fulfil that role.

11

Varieties of Gifts, Varieties of Service (part 1)

'Christ is like a single body which has many parts, it is still one body, even though it is made up of different parts.'
(1 Corinthians 12: 12)

What do Deacons do? That is the question that is often asked and that's the question Deacons find impossible to answer. We can talk about enabling, encouraging, pioneering, being people of vision, being involved at the margins; but to define a role is impossible as no two Deacons do the same work. 'Varieties of gifts and varieties of service' was a phrase used in the centenary year and in many ways it sums up the varied work undertaken by Deacons. This chapter shares a few icons of ministry from different periods, telling some incredible stories of incredible people who minister quietly at the margins.

Over the years the work of a number of Deaconesses has been recognised by the state with an MBE award: Edith McBeth DCS for her work with Huts and Canteens; Mary Rhind DCS for her work in Corby; Ellen Rutherford DCS for her work at Strathconan; Nancy Copland DCS and Norma Ronald DCS both for prison work. Alice Scrimgeour DCS was named 'Scotswomen of the Year'; Helen Hughes DCS was given a 'Community Saint' award.

Maureen Hutchison (Mathieson)

Maureen was a member of Trinity Duke Street Church and as a young person had always been encouraged by her minister the Rev.

91

Denis Duncan. She was a member of the Girls' Association and had worked for an organisation within the Christian Institute in Glasgow before going to St Colm's in 1958.

On completion of her training she went to St Thomas Church, Leith, where she was commissioned in 1961. It was there she met Ian Hutchison whom she was later to marry. She went to St Mungo's, Cumbernauld, in 1968. Maureen was a great people person and could get the life stories out of people as she went about the parish.

In 1972 she married Ian in St Thomas's, Leith. She had to resign her position as at that time Deaconesses were not allowed to continue after marriage. However as there were more placements for Deaconesses than people available, Maureen was approached by the Home Board and invited to return part-time: so she became the first married Deaconess.

In 1973 she was appointed to the Old Kirk, West Pilton. She became a well known figure in the area going up and down stairs that others avoided, as she reached out to folk in need. She was linked to a Presbyterial Council of the Woman's Guild in the Borders where she became well known, receiving support for her work from Guilds who provided supplies for her famous 'food cupboard'. Maureen knew about feeding the hungry. Clothes were also given for the local thrift shop run ecumenically by the churches in the greater Pilton area. She was well known and loved in Church and community in the area. The congregation benefited from Maureen's wisdom and experience; as did the ministers and many assistants and students for both ministry and the Diaconate she worked with.

For ten years before her retirement, Maureen served in Granton Parish Church and then she joined Ian in worshipping at St Thomas's, where she was very much a confidant and support to the ministers. She always spoke her mind and was respected for it.

Ellen Rutherford

Ellen Rutherford was commissioned on 11 May 1962. At an early age she felt called to the Church first as a female minister, then as a missionary doctor; however ill health was to hinder her progress. Eventually her mother suggested she might become a Deaconess but she was turned down because she was not strong enough to cope with tenement stairs. This was to be the story of Ellen's life. Each time she felt called to some work, health prevented her. Eventually she found her life's work at Strathconon Manse. In her book *Loaves and Fishes* (1998) she describes how thousands of young people from all walks of life and all corners of the earth found their way along the twisty miles of road to Strathconon Manse. Her story, too, had its twists and turns.

Ellen began teacher training in Dundee in 1939 and because of the war she found herself teaching small groups of children in kitchens or small rural schools; she was also involved with youth clubs. At the centenary celebrations for David Livingstone she learned of the need for people to help train teachers for small African Schools. She did a relief placement at Straloch and then was appointed as head teacher although she had not applied for the position. In due course she applied to the Foreign Mission Committee with a view of going to Africa to train teachers; once again, however, she was turned down on the grounds of poor health.

She taught for eighteen years, mainly in single teacher schools, learning how to do basic repairs as the school houses were all in a bad state of repair with primitive or non-existent plumbing, dry rot and roofs needing repairs. On Sundays she trailed a caravan around Loch Rannoch conducting Sunday Schools. She spoke at Guilds and took the occasional church service. When a new school was to be built at Rannoch, she wondered once again, at 42, if she could work in the Church. She checked her finances to see if she could afford the fees at St Colm's for a year. Her financial commitments made it impossible.

A visit to the area by the General Secretary of the Youth Committee led to Ellen meeting him to ask for a job. It turned out that her experience of running rural schools was just what he was looking for: someone to train women willing to have Sunday schools in their own home. Going to Edinburgh for an interview, she was told she could work with senior youth as well as with rural Sunday Schools in the Synod of Ross. At the expense of the Youth Committee, she was sent to St Colm's to train as a Deaconess. Before she went to train, she needed a home (no longer being a teacher she would lose her school house) and at first was told there was nowhere available; then Ellen was offered Strathconon Manse, though it was in a bad state of repair. On going to see this dilapidated place she wondered if this was really where God wanted her to be. The story of Gideon's fleece came to her mind and looking up the story in Bible the words hit her *'Have not I sent thee?'* She went to St Colm's.

At the beginning of the second term she heard that the Senior Youth Committee's regulations had changed: to work with them would now mean an additional course at Moray House to get a diploma. Study and the move to Strathconan had left her emotionally drained: she was too weary to do another course. Without the diploma she could not work with senior youth; so yet another Committee of the Church had turned her down. She was, however, allowed to do Sunday School teacher training. The Deaconess Committee, which had originally accepted her as a candidate, now said she could not be commissioned when she finished her training as they had decided her previous experience was not a sufficient qualification for becoming a Deaconess.

Ellen returned to Strathconon in January 1962, completely dejected and suffering from depression; and her mother took ill and died. In spite of being at a low ebb Ellen still felt that God was calling her. Going up the road one stormy night she offered the house and the furniture to God as her *'loaves and fishes'* and asked Him somehow to use them to feed a multitude with *'the bread of life'*. She decided to leave everything to God; if young people came of their own accord, she would know it was what God wanted. In the meantime – opinions having again changed – she was commissioned as a Deaconess to do Sunday School work.

In August with things at their lowest ebb – failed plumbing, dripping pipes – a knock came to the door and three drenched young men stood there. They had been washed out of their camp and one of them remembered a work camp he had come to at Strathconon and asked if they could stay. They mended the pipes and later were to return with others: from there things snowballed. Soon folk started to turn up at Strathconon from all over the British Isles and over 50 countries. Electricians, plumbers, joiners, builders, would often arrive complete with the materials needed. Gradually the whole house was transformed and the bothy was made into a little chapel – all done voluntarily.

In time folks gathered round the kitchen table from all walks of life, backgrounds, cultures and countries. They would ask how it all started and Ellen would tell them how on a dark and stormy night she had offered '*her loaves and fishes to God*'.

Stella Reekie

The Rt. Hon. The Lord Provost of Glasgow Michael Kelly in a
forward to a book about Stella Reekie[xxiii] said that Glasgow owed an
incalculable debt to her for her efforts to break down barriers and
build understanding between people. Balwant Singh Saggu, the
leader of the Sikh community, spoke from his heart at a gathering to
celebrate her life, when he said:[xxiv]

> '*Stella Reekie was too great for me. I could not grasp
> her: I could not understand her. I did not understand
> what was meant by saying 'Jesus died for our sins'.
> Now I do understand what it means, Stella died for us.
> She suffered for us ... so that we the Hindus, Sikhs,
> Muslims, Bahais, Jews, Christians and others could get
> together and learn to live in love, peace and harmony.
> For the Christians she was a Christian but she was
> something more than that. To me she was like water,
> clear running water. If you pour it into a glass it takes
> the shape of the glass; if you pour it into a flask, it takes
> the shape of the flask. She became the shape of what
> was needed at anytime where she was. For me a Sikh,
> Stella was a Sikh. ... She was a saint of God and
> showed what the love of God was like.*'

Stella Reekie was commissioned as a Deaconess in Woodlands
Church 28 January 1971. It was said she put on her grey uniform and
badge at her commissioning and wore them with pride thereafter.
Stella came from Kent where she had trained as a Nursery Nurse.
After the war she went with the Red Cross to Belsen in Germany to
work with children. In 1949 she went to St Colm's to train for two
years before going to work in Pakistan in response to a request for a
Bible Woman.

Stella was to serve in Pakistan for seventeen years. It was while she
was there she began to practise the hospitality for which she was to

become famous. She was described as having an iron will and undeviating courage in many difficult situations.

On her return from Pakistan she worked for a time in Wishaw with a refugee rehabilitation project before taking up a joint appointment with the YWCA and the Church of Scotland working amongst overseas families in Glasgow. A flat was acquired and it became an open house for people of many different backgrounds and communities. Later she was to move into a double flat in Glasgow Street which became the centre of many projects in the area. The 'Sharing of Faiths project' developed into an annual 'Presentation of Faiths' event. Father Gerry Hughes writing a letter after Stella's death said '*When I think of holiness I think of Stella*'. Maxwell Craig said that one of Stella's more remarkable gifts was her ability to ask her friends for more than they were prepared to give. Her work at the International Flat in Glasgow drew many people from many different cultures and traditions: at the flat they could come together as one.

Helen Hughes

Helen Hughes trained at St Colm's from 1973-75. This was followed by a year of specialised training which was spent working as a Social Work Assistant with Lothian Regional Council. She was appointed to St. Paul's Church, Johnstone in 1976 where she served a probationary year before being commissioned in 1977. During the time she was there, much of the local industry came to an end, resulting in growing unemployment. Her roles in the parish included pastoral work, housegroups for elderly church members, school work, Bible Class, weekly visits to the Playtex Factory, and helping on the rota for a breakfast shelter for homeless people in Paisley.

In 1980 she was appointed to Lansdowne Church, Glasgow, an old Victorian Church situated in the west end of the city. Her duties included pastoral work, and she began to conduct funerals, as well as working with children in school and church; involvement with an ecumenical community care scheme which provided volunteer visitors for elderly people; a monthly coffee morning; and organising occasional outings. She also coordinated a weekly soup run to George Square with the Simon Community, and served on the management committee of Maryhill Community Central Hall, which included being on the advisory group for the local Travellers and Gypsy Project. She had occasional involvement in the leading of worship and would work with a group of people to lead the worship when holiday cover for her minister was needed.

Involvement in the soup run in Lansdowne Parish led to concern for youth destitution, and the formation of a group of people from local churches of different denominations to consider how they could respond to the problem. Eventually it led to the formation of the West End Churches Key Fund, a rent deposit scheme to enable single homeless people to access housing with private landlords. This project has since grown and developed and is now the Glasgow Rent Deposit and Support Scheme, a city wide project, which still has church members as directors. The Board is currently chaired by a member of one of the original churches, and works in partnership with voluntary agencies, including the Simon Community, Barnardo's Faith and Community Project and the YMCA. Helen described it as an excellent experience working with others through the process of sharing a concern, finding a vision, and working to bring this vision into reality.

In 2002 Helen was appointed to two churches: Springburn Parish, an area of deprivation in the north of Glasgow; and Tron St. Mary's Parish, which included the Red Road flats where large numbers of people seeking asylum in Scotland were housed. In Springburn parish she was involved in school work and pastoral work, including the regular visitation of housebound members, the conduct of funerals and worship in a home for elderly people. In Tron St. Mary's parish, her role was to support people who were asylum seekers or refugees. This support included an English class, a parent and toddler's group, and an after-school drop-in for children and their parents. She also spent time visiting people in their homes, supporting people through their claims for asylum, and through health and family difficulties.

In each parish where she served there was a good balance of church with community work, but there was always a strong emphasis on community outreach and being alongside those living on the margins of society. She valued this aspect and counted it a great privilege to get to know some amazing people who struggled through very difficult situations, whether it was homelessness, or having had to flee from their own home and country to seek refuge here and encounter all sorts of new problems as they battled their way through the asylum system. Through the Church, Helen sought to welcome people into church and community, and found herself being welcomed into people's homes and lives, which was a great privilege. In retirement many of these doors are still open to her and she has become an adopted 'granny' to two little girls whose Mum she first met when she came as an asylum seeker from Burundi and who has now settled in Glasgow.

Ann Lyall

Ann began her training at St Ninian's, Crieff, doing the Training in Evangelism Course and this was followed by two years at St Colm's. At the end of this she did a year at Hamilton College of Education doing the Teacher Training Post Graduate Primary Course.

While at St Ninian's, a three month placement in Galashiels involved her in visiting new houses, the housebound and elderly, as well as being involved in the life of the congregation and youth work. Her studies at St Ninian's included Biblical Studies and Church History as well as participating in the life of the Centre and working with groups who came. The students also did two week missions in various parts of Scotland, working alongside the local church and helping them with their programme for mission.

Her time at St Colm's was a very positive experience for her with its communal living, daily worship, weekly presentations and practical work placements. Through the presentations, team work was encouraged, bringing out imaginative presentation styles, providing opportunities to work with different people. The practical placements (eight hours in the first year and 20 hours in the second) presented challenges and experiences of different aspects which Ann, left to herself, might not have chosen, such as an open door Youth Club. In her second year she was challenged by the broad base of theological thinking. As well as the 20 hour placements there was a week in Hospital Chaplaincy and time with Industrial Chaplains. During her second year some students were allowed to experiment with small group living, in a house owned by the College. The second year students organised and participated in a week long retreat.

At Hamilton College she stayed in Halls of Residence which was a very different and isolating experience but helped to prepare her for living on her own in a parish. The teacher training – concentrating on RE, getting practical experience in two primary schools, one special primary for children with learning needs and one secondary school – was helpful for her work as a Deaconess.

Ann worked with National Mission in Castlemilk East from September 1979 until December 2002. A large housing scheme, it was one of four schemes built in Glasgow after the war to house people who had lived in overcrowded conditions in places like the Gorbals. The schemes were built with no facilities, only houses, and soon developed problems. By the time Ann arrived in Castlemilk it was an area of multiple deprivation with a high crime rate, notorious for its street gangs and vandalism. Unemployment was high and the level of poverty got worse as the Thatcher years took hold. Single parent families were on the rise, glue sniffing was the main problem, drugs were on the way and were soon to become a major player in the streets of Castlemilk.

For the 23 years she worked there she was part of a team as Parish Assistant. In the beginning George Pirie the Lay Missionary did a lot of the pastoral work, funerals and preaching while her main work was education. As a team they had the chaplaincy of six schools. She visited schools two or three times a week taking part in Assemblies and classes, over the years getting to know hundreds of children.

In the life of the congregation she was involved in building up the leadership of the Church through Sunday School and teacher training. Youth work involved taking teenagers away for weekends, encouraging them to be involved in city and national events. Other work included the Open Door Youth Club, a Care of the Old Group and the Friendship Club. She also organised holidays to Craigengower; took groups to Iona and youth groups and family groups to the Badenoch Centre. Encouraging people to participate in the worship led to setting up a worship group. Visiting folk at home, in hospital and in homes; helping to lead the Bible Study and House Groups; and attending Board and Session meetings were also part of her work.

There was a strong ecumenical movement in Castlemilk involving 10 churches which led to Ecumenical Services, Lent Groups, Easter Pilgrimages, special prayer events, Retreat Days and the monthly meeting for the full time staff. When asylum seekers first started arriving in Castlemilk in 2000, an Ecumenical Refugee Centre was set up and supported by all the churches; Ann was involved in various ways. Other community involvement included the Castlemilk Law Centre, being member and chair of various School Boards, involvement with the Pensioners Action Centre, and Victims Support.

After George Pirie's retirement, Ann was more involved in leading worship, funerals and pastoral care; work, she felt, that was more like being a minister than a Deacon. While gaining a higher profile she felt it was less Diaconal. At Presbytery level she served on the Parish Education Committee for 20 years and was very involved in the youth work of the Presbytery organising various events and supporting the Youth Advisor for Presbytery.

The majority of Ann's work in Castlemilk was Church based, building up the people of God for the work of God within the community, creating a worshipping base and a supportive, enabling fellowship.

On leaving Castlemilk, Ann served as Chaplain at the Lodging House Mission situated in the Calton area of Glasgow. The Mission catered for the homeless community of the city. People came from across the city, the country and from overseas. If the people of Castlemilk were at the bottom of the ladder, she said those she met in the Mission had fallen off. Her main responsibilities there were pastoral care, providing worship and prayers and also Christian Education to those who went to the mission. She also had a responsibility for going into the community to the hostels and streets where homeless people were. She liaised with the Church at large, keeping them informed of the work, looking for support and helping to integrate homeless people back into their local church community. As a Chaplain she found her role very different from that at Castlemilk and had to learn sometimes do nothing in order to leave space to be available for people when they needed her.

A new challenge presented itself when Ann was appointed as one of two peripatetic Deacons. Her first appointment was to Lochaber Presbytery for eighteen months and then to Lanark Presbytery for over two years where she has been working across eight different congregations. In both situations she was involved in helping congregations through a time of transition and change. She is now part of the Interim Ministry team in the Church of Scotland.

Pat Munro

Pat Munro became President of Diaconate Council in June 2013.

After graduating from Strathclyde University in 1971 she moved to Aberdeen to take a Teaching Certificate. It was in Aberdeen that she started attending the Church of Scotland (having been brought up in the Congregational Church). After one year she moved to Perth to teach at Perth Grammar School where she taught Mathematics and Religious Education. She attended and became a member of the North Church in Perth and taught in Sunday School and became involved in Youth Work and, later on, Summer Mission.

After seven years teaching, she moved to a large insurance company based in Perth and after a few years arranged a transfer to work with the same company in Philadelphia, USA, where she attended a Presbyterian Church. While there, she began seriously to question what she wanted to spend her life doing. She assumed the only jobs available with the Church meant being a minister or a missionary. She had been aware that the church in which she had been involved had the need of some kind of assistance for the minister with a membership of 1,500 and a large parish. She wrote to the minister who directed her to write to the Board of Ministry and Mission.

After much thought and prayer she decided to return to Scotland. Folk she spoke to in Scotland made comments like 'So you are going to be a Deaconess then'. She had never heard of Deaconesses! When she went to the church offices for a chat she was asked 'Are you sure you don't want to be a minister, after all you already have a degree?' She didn't believe God was calling her to be a minister and when she heard about the Deaconesses she realised that was what she wanted to be in spite of the complex relationship between employing committees and the Diaconate. She was only required to do one year at St Colm's.

On completion of her training she felt called to the North Church in Perth but the Board were not too happy about sending someone back to a congregation they had been a member of. However after much thought on their part and much prayer on hers, she began work as a Probationer Deaconess in 1985 and was commissioned on 5 November 1986.

Pat's work in Perth was in many ways new, as folks there had no preconceived notion of what a Deaconess would do. She was mainly to be responsible for outreach work in the parish, quickly becoming involved in the Primary School. In the church she was involved in pastoral visitation and some worship. She said she would never preach; however she eventually did preach and lead worship taking responsibility for the all-age service when it started.

When Deacons and Deaconesses were given their place in the courts of the Church, Pat became the first Deaconess appointed as Moderator of a Presbytery in the Church of Scotland, in Perth, 1999-2000.

It was a surprise to her when she saw a job advertised for a Deacon at St Columba's Church in London and felt drawn to it. After much agonising, tears and prayer, she left the North Church in August 2001 and started at St Columba's, Pont Street, on 1st September that year. She was ordained as a Deacon in St Columba's. Her main responsibilities were pastoral work; weekly involvement in worship; and outreach work with the homeless alongside other West London Churches. She was Moderator of the Presbytery of England 2005-2006.

Pat was appointed to Lochgelly St Serf's and Ballingry in 2007, eighty years after the first team ministry in the Lochgelly area, and began her current position in St John's and St Leonard's Church, Perth, in 2012.

John Buchanan

John Buchanan was the last person to train as a Lay Missionary. When at the end of the 1970s the Home Board had limited funding to train students, St Colm's College developed the Church and Community Course which was open to people who wanted to study independently. John responded to the Advert in *Life & Work* and was the first independent student to take the course at St Colm's 1980-81.

At end of the year he applied to the Home Board and was accepted to do a second year to complete the course in Diaconal Ministry. At that time although previous conversations had taken place between the Diaconate and the Lay Missionaries, the Lay Missionaries had decided not to go down the route of becoming Deacons. When John applied it was assumed by the employing Committee he would be a Lay Missionary because he was male.

He was appointed to Rosyth and was commissioned as a Lay Missionary in 1983 by Dunfermline Presbytery. John became a Deacon in 1988 along with sixteen other Lay Missionaries. From Rosyth John served for ten years in St Andrew's and St Stephen's Riverside Parish, Perth, as it moved to the new church building. His final appointment was to St Clement's and St Ninian's, Musselburgh, before his retirement. One important thing for John as a Deacon is the fact his calling continues into retirement, enjoying the fellowship of fellow Deacons.

Joyce Mitchell

'So that's a Deaconess – what a wonderful sort of person!' That was
Joyce Mitchell's reaction after first meeting with Ellen Rutherford as
Ellen gathered up and packed into her little van the wealth of helpful
materials she had brought to show a very new, struggling, Sunday
School teacher. Joyce's minister had suggested she talk with a
Deaconess who worked fairly near-by as someone who could help
her. She had never heard of such a person before. After an afternoon
of Ellen's encouragement, finding out Joyce's interests and abilities
and pointing out how she could use them, Joyce began to believe she
could actually do the job of Sunday School teaching.

Some time later, when she joined the Woman's Guild, she heard of
another Deaconess: Norma Ronald, for whom they were asked to
collect and send toiletries, to distribute to the inmates of Cornton
Vale Prison where she was a chaplain.

This, then, was Joyce's only knowledge of Deaconesses. It was some
time later, after a sermon which her minister preached on Moses and
the burning bush, that she began to consider God's call to her. She,
like Moses, made excuses but still one word came to her:
'Deaconess'. Her family had grown up and left home and a certain
restlessness had set in. She felt she should be doing something more,
but what? She was half way through the T.L.S. course[xxv] which her
minister had encouraged her to do, when she experienced a very
definite call to be a Deaconess. After the usual enquiries and
attending selection school she found herself embarking in 1991 on a
two year course at St. Colm's. The residential training was ideal for
her. She said she could not have concentrated on the course work
without being separated from local church involvements, domestic
responsibilities and other distractions.

She enjoyed the broad spectrum of academic and practical study and
experience at St Colm's as well as establishing good habits of prayer
and quiet times. She learned the nature of Diaconal and team

ministry and was exposed to a variety of different theologies. Having enjoyed the teaching of Ken Lawson at St. Colm's she did a further course on Transactional Analysis based on Jean Morrison's books, 'A Tool for Christians'.

Another workshop Joyce attended was led by Olive Drane on Christian clowning and she became one of the 'Celtic Christian Clowns', touring each other's churches bringing a different way of looking at the Gospel. They also took part in bigger events, such as the Scottish Christian Gathering and the 50th anniversary of Christian Aid.

The ministry of healing had long been an interest of Joyce so she attended a number of the Social Responsibility's conferences, and developed a healing group, open to all, in the church of Holy Trinity, Wester Hailes, where she was appointed on completion of her training. She took study leave to do the course of 'Training in Faith Accompaniment' and two years later a follow up on 'Training in Spiritual Direction'.

Wester Hailes had a population of 11,000 population and had a bad reputation in the past as a deprived area with problems relating to drugs and violence. Joyce's long involvement in the parish enabled her to form links with other agencies and projects in the area, often sharing the care and support of the vulnerable and needy. Prison visiting brought new opportunities. The church café grew and as it developed over the years it became Joyce's responsibility to see that all the volunteers got suitable food hygiene training to comply with all the new regulations. She set up a pastoral visiting team and trained one member of the congregation in the conduct of funerals; she also trained people to participate in worship.

Both Council and local Deaconess groups are important to Joyce to meet not only those still 'active' but also the retired. The older 'Deacs' had been an inspiration to her in her ministry. She greatly enjoyed and benefited from the retreat days which were a time of refreshing and refocusing. Knowing that she is part of a world-wide fellowship of people with a common ethos, purpose and vision is special for her. She says there is a great sense of security and supportedness in this and also a privilege to belong to such a community. She still finds it hard to believe she was called to be a Deaconess and remembers that first meeting with Ellen Rutherford and thinking what a wonderful kind of person! She says, '*I'm sure the Lord had a chuckle knowing the plans He had for me!*'

In her retirement Joyce returned to the north and hopes to develop her garden as a 'Quiet Garden' and place of retreat for those who need time and space apart.

Jean Porter

Jean Porter (Clark) says '*My story is not remarkable – but it has often seemed that I have been a forerunner on this journey – or should that be guinea pig?*'

Her journey to Diaconal ministry began at the age of 9 when she announced to her mother that she wanted to be a Deaconess, her inspiration being Miss Nan Muir DCS, the Parish Deaconess. From that day on the desire to serve God as a Deaconess never left her, though her life took many twists and turns.

The journey proper began when she learned of a pilot Enquiry Conference. The Church hoped the new Enquiry Process would channel people into service within the Church, in a way which would test their sense of calling while affirming them as individuals. At the conference, those who expressed an interest in becoming Deacons were told that at that point the Church did not know how it would train its Deacons, nor how it would use them once trained – but that it could involve a three year BD course.

She says '*For someone who appreciates certainty and who likes to know in advance what's about to happen, this was not good news. Despite this, I remained convinced that this was God's plan for me – and if it took a BD to become a Deacon, so be it*'. She began a six month accompaniment process with a minister. At the end of the six months, a review was held involving representatives from Ministries Council, Presbytery, the minister and herself. The purpose of the review was to determine whether she should pursue the call to Diaconal ministry. The outcome of the review was very positive and so she applied for training as a Deacon. She attended a selection conference in August 2001, in Dundee. If successful her training was to consist of a three year BD course plus placements. The placements would consist of one term-time part-time placement, a summer full-time placement for three months and a year's probationary period. There would also be a conference programme: four years in total.

She was accepted for training but was also told there would be no guarantee of work at the end of the training. In faith she gave up her work, not sure if she would qualify for a grant. Jean enjoyed her training at New College studying alongside Word and Sacrament candidates. The conference programme put demands on her as a single parent as it was residential. However it was a valuable part of the programme: building relationships and respect, giving an insight on Diaconal ministry to Word and Sacrament students and *vice versa*. She saw gradual changes in what been very much a Word and Sacrament-based conference programme to being more inclusive of Diaconal ministry. Attending Diaconate Council in January and in June were important parts of their training: meeting with active and retired Deacons, learning from their experience.

Jean's placements were all with ministers as there were no Deacons in her Presbytery. During her third year at New College, she was given the opportunity to do a 10-week practical hospital placement at Edinburgh Royal Infirmary as part of a Pastoral Care and Theology Course under the supervision of Ann Mulligan DCS.

Looking back, Jean is grateful for the training she received. The BD provided a solid theological base from which to go out in service, providing the tools for theological reflection in Diaconal ministry. She found, too, that to challenge and be challenged by Word and Sacrament candidates on their ideas and beliefs on theology in general and ministry in particular was one of the most rewarding aspects of the BD course. The one thing she would change would be to provide a set course/conference material on the history of the Diaconate.

At the end of the probationary period it took time to find a placement as she was only allowed to apply for one place at a time. When she was appointed to Robroyston, she was the first Deacon to be actually ordained in Glasgow Presbytery. It was while she was there she was to meet her future husband.

Jean's journey began by being inspired by Nan Muir DCS, who was involved in children's work and family ministry in Tullibody, Clackmannanshire. Her work now has brought her back to the same Presbytery to St Mark's in Stirling where she is involved in worship, pastoral, ecumenical and community work as well as schools chaplaincy. Jean is reminded of the saying:

'*God moves behind the scenes*
And he moves the scenes He is behind.'

12

Varieties of Gifts, Varieties of Service (part 2)

'There are different kinds of spiritual gifts, but the same Spirit gives them. There are different ways of serving but the same Lord is served.'
(1 Corinthians 12: 4-5)

The breadth of our story is not complete without mention of vocations served in their own distinct areas of mission and outreach, alongside the more usual Diaconal ministry to community and parish.

And of course, besides those who worked for the Home Board (and its successors), there were those who were for a time with the Youth Committee – for example Norma Ronald, Margaret Cameron, Elma Sloan and Sheila Moyes in the 1960s. (Elma worked as a Sunday School organizer and in the 70s was to work for the Overseas Council as Partner Plan Secretary and later as Home Organisation Secretary. Sheila went on to be General Secretary of the Young Women's Christian Association.) Deacons have had posts with the Board of Social Responsibility now Crossreach – Elspeth McPheat (many stories too numerous to tell); as Hospital Chaplains Assistants: Ann Mulligan and Ann McDonald; or those who worked with the hard of hearing: Dorothy Malvenan, Phyllis Gillon, Elsie Miller. Space does not allow for the many stories covering the variety of work undertaken by Deacons, some of whom served for a period of time and went into the ministry of Word and Sacrament, saying they were better Ministers for their time spent in the Diaconate. Diaconal ministry in Scotland has been marked by innovation and service; flexibility and mobility have been its keynotes.

Margaret Howden

Margaret Howden trained at St Colm's in 1952-53. She had worked with the Church of Scotland Huts and Canteens in Orkney during the war years, then went on to do a leadership course at Moray House. She had two youth leadership posts before going to work as Secretary of The Girls' Association. While at St Colm's she did additional classes at Moray House in Christian Education and Nursery School with practical work at Simpson House, on preparation for Sunday School teachers.

Margaret was appointed as Sunday School Organiser for the Synod of Fife in 1953. Commissioned as a Deaconess the following year she was to serve with the Education Committee until 1977 covering four Presbyteries as Sunday School Organiser. Reports were sent to the Director of the Education Committee at the Church of Scotland Offices. Her work involved her working with Sunday Schools Youth Conveners and Committees. She ran training courses for Sunday School teachers.

In Dunfermline and Kirkcaldy Presbyteries elementary and intermediate certificates were awarded to young people who attended the eight-week courses and passed a written test. Before she finished working she felt Ministers were sending less able young people for training; though Grace Clark, one of the young people who attended training, was later to train as a Deaconess.

In the 70s and 80s she also ran adult education courses in the Dunfermline and Kirkcaldy Presbyteries.

Margaret had a Mobile Training Unit which was used in particularly rural areas. Sometime she was sent to remote Presbyteries for two to three weeks as well as leading Sunday School teacher summer schools at Bonskeid and St Andrews. The work also included Sunday School Union Conventions in various parts of the country and she was involved in planning the Sunday School Union Lesson Schemes in Glasgow. Latterly she led some of the National Sunday School

Teacher weekend courses at Carberry Tower at Musselburgh. It was there I was first to meet Margaret as a young Primary leader and later as a Deaconess I was to become involved with her in planning and running these weekends.

On her resignation as Sunday School Organiser in 1977, Margaret went to India for two five-month spells doing voluntary work. She did an eight-week residential course in counselling and went on to use the healing energy she had in her hands both in a hospital in India and when she came home. In 1981 she spent some time in Jamaica doing voluntary work before returning to Kirkcaldy where in her retirement she taught English as a second language for 14 years.

Kay Ramsay

During the 60s and 70s Kay Ramsay was part-time Secretary to the Deaconess Board as well as being involved in parish placements. Kay grew up at Dalkeith Road in Edinburgh attending school at Gillespies where she was a star pupil in English and Literature. This was to stand her in good stead for the paths she was to take.

In 1944 she was called up for war work, two years into her degree course at Edinburgh University. She was sent to British Piston Rings Ltd at Gorgie where she measured piston rings for Bristol Bombers. It was extremely boring work and after eight months she was suffering from exhaustion. She was next sent as assistant cataloguer in Edinburgh University Library which she described as 'sheer bliss'. She remained there until the end of the war and was able to recommence her studies. After graduating in 1948 she was librarian at Grassland Research Station, Stratford upon Avon where having a passion for Shakespeare she went to all the plays. It was there she first felt that God was calling her to serve Him but not quite then. In 1950 she achieved her ambition to be a newspaper reporter and until 1955 served on the Montrose Review, the Alloa Journal, and the Ayr Advertiser before answering a call to enquire about Deaconess work.

Kay started training at St Colm's in 1955. She was commissioned in 1958 as one of the last under the old order of service and one of the first to wear the new charcoal grey uniform. She was appointed to St James, Pollock. She was to go on to serve in St Andrew's Clermiston; Granton; and Holy Trinity before going in 1980 to work with the Board of World Mission where she was responsible for the archives as well as editing newspapers and having responsibility for overseas bursars.

In 1963 she was appointed as Secretary to the Deaconess Board. It was Kay who described the 60s and 70s as the Diaconate's 'Years of Struggle'. She had a vision for the Church of Scotland having a Diaconate that was not the lowest step in the hierarchy (as it was in the other great Churches of the world) but on a level with both the Ministers and the laity, acting as a bridge enabling Ministers and laity to relate together. However each time a scheme was brought to the Assembly it was knocked back. She said when ordination was mentioned in 1974 it split the Church in two and took the stuffing out of the scheme. She said they drew in their horns then until Professor T. F. Torrance encouraged them with his paper stating the Diaconate was a 'ministry of response to the word of God'. In 1977 when they suggested all servants of the Church should be paid out of the same fund, the report was met with 'a deafening silence'. Kay's impression of the relationship with National Mission at this time was that the Diaconate was 'a bit of a nuisance'. However Kay's clear and open thinking and her wide reading and knowledge of the Church made her a lynchpin during those difficult years. From 1982 to 85 she was President of the Diaconate Council and Vice Convener of the Diaconate Committee.

Kay made a major contribution on the world scene serving as English editor of the World Federation *Diakonia News* from 1973 to 1988. To celebrate 50 years of DIAKONIA she edited *Diakonia Challenge and Response*[xxvi] which traced the path of the world conferences and the individuals involved. She was present at the book launch in Friedrichroda in 1996.

After retiring from World Mission, Kay trained in Spiritual Direction and was involved in the retreat movement. She organised retreat days for her fellow Deacons for many years as well as writing reflective Biblical narratives for the Newsletter. She was an Associate of the Catholic Society for the Sacred Heart and was part of a pastoral team of the L'Arche Community. When she ceased parish work she joined Richmond Craigmillar Church and became an active member and great support to all who ministered there. Right to the end she was leading a meditation group at Homeroyal House, which had been her home after leaving Dalkeith Road.

Helen Thom

Helen trained at St Colm's from 1956 -58. The experience of communal living, studies and practical work was one which all the students benefited from. There was also the spiritual enrichment from morning and evening prayers led by staff and students in the quiet chapel, with the stained glass window, featuring the risen Christ with the sword and the light against a background of faraway lands. Events within the life of the College were recorded by the senior student, sometimes in a humorous vein, others quite brief, and read out at House Guild on a Monday morning.

There were summer assignments to the berry-pickers and also visits to churches on the continent to view their work and outreach, enlarging the vision of the world wide Church. Life long friendships were also formed with overseas candidates.

Helen's time at St Colm's was an all round experience equipping her for work as a probationer at Cardonald Parish Church where she served four years. She was commissioned in April 1959. She preached at occasional services in Cardonald and she herself was challenged while preaching on the text from John 12: 24 – '*Unless a grain of wheat falls to the ground and dies, it remains only a single seed. But if it dies, it produces many seeds*' – that she felt called to the mission field. The Church of Scotland mission in South Arabia was looking for a woman evangelist to work among women. So in 1962 she returned to St Colm's for one term missionary training before leaving in February 1963 for six months study of Arabic in Beirut, Lebanon, before appointment to Aden.

The main outreach of the Church of Scotland mission in Aden was at the Affara Hospital. Her work was mainly with the women and children. The women came to the clinic at the hospital with their sick babies. Many babies were malnourished and underweight. One baby weighed only 7 pounds at 7 months old. Her mother did not love her because she looked like a stick. However she made daily visits to receive powdered milk, paid for by an Edinburgh Sunday School and with 'TLC' became a healthy baby and her mother began to love her too. One girl went to the Friday Girls' Club and listened intently to the Bible Stories; but her father was an Imam at one of the mosques and it wasn't long before she stopped going.

The fight for independence began in the Yemen in 1963. Aden had been a British Colony since 1937 and for four years there were three different nationalist parties fighting for power. Mission work was curtailed and moved to the Beihan station although Helen remained at Affara. Before independence was granted in 1967 and the country became known as the Peoples' Republic of Southern Yemen, a state of emergency had been declared and missionary staff were withdrawn.

Some time later former Arab staff wrote to the Overseas Council asking for the return of the missionaries. Most missionaries returned in 1968 but after a few years in 1972 requests for permits were denied and staff had to return home bringing 86 years of mission work to an end. Through the difficulties, '*Traditions which Endure*', the little booklet with the lectionary of daily readings from Psalms which had been a feature of St Colm's, gave her the endurance and strength to go.

Helen had hoped that she might be able to return to the Yemen as a teacher in Government service; so with this in mind she did a year at Telford College, followed by a three year University BA, and a one year Diploma in Teaching at Moray House. However by the time she qualified the door to the Yemen had closed completely. She began teaching at Ainslie Park School, Edinburgh.

While Helen had been overseas she was on the Supplementary list of Deaconesses but she still felt herself to be a Deaconess. Now restored to the Active list, while employed with Lothian Region she found it was more difficult to think of herself as a Deaconess, feeling cut off from the business of local groups and Council as a Deaconess in secular employment. For Helen it was the employment within the Church and being subject to its discipline which gave authenticity to being a Deaconess, together with being within the fellowship of the

Diaconate. While others may have seen it differently, it was her experience which influenced her thinking.

Alison Cunningham

Alison Cunningham trained at Westhill Training College, Selly Oak, Birmingham for two years, 1948–50. She completed one of the earliest Youth and Community courses. Later Scottish Church History was covered by attending classes run by Dr James Bulloch.

She joined the Youth Committee as Sunday School Organiser and was first sent to the Presbytery of Dumfries. She had a two year break to look after her grandmother before serving with the Synod of Merse and Teviotdale for ten years. It was during this time she decided to apply to become a Deaconess and was commissioned on 14 November 1961 in the Parish Church of Bowden. It was a great privilege for her in the Centenary year to address her fellow Deaconesses at a service in Bowden – the church where both she and Lady Grisell Baillie had been commissioned.

Her next placement took her to Dundee where she served an area stretching from just south of Aberdeen to Stirling, after which she was moved to Glasgow Presbytery for five years before finishing work with the Youth Committee.

Retaining her status as a Deaconess she went to work with Renfrewshire County Council as one of the first two Community Development Officers within the Social Work Department. She was appointed to the Eastwood District on the south side of Glasgow where she was to do some of her most lasting and worthwhile work bringing Church and Community together. Later, an invitation to the celebration of the 25th anniversary of the voluntary day centres for housebound people, was a reminder of how that work had continued as evidence of all she had done in that part of her life.

On retiral Alison nursed her mother for a time, after her death she was invited to be part-time General Secretary of the Scottish Sunday School Union. She served for six years and during this time was involved with her colleagues in delivering correspondence courses for Sunday School teachers. In her time of training Sunday School teachers she had tried to raise the awareness of the importance of Christian education, which she saw as the Cinderella of the Church.

After this her activities were based in the Milngavie community. When she finally retired it was in a congregation with sufficient talent and human resources to allow her to sit back with an easy conscience.

Jean C. Morrison (nee Grigor)

A primary school teacher before going to St Colm's, Jean became a parish Deaconess in Castlemilk, Glasgow. In 1968 Jean was granted a year's World Council of Churches Scholarship to study Adult Christian Education in Chicago Theological Seminary, USA. This introduced her to Pastoral Psychology (not then available in the U.K.) which was to change and inform the future focus of her Diaconal ministry. On her return to Glasgow she trained leaders and set up house groups in the parish, to help people get to know and support each other: one was for those who couldn't physically access the church building.

A letter from Australia invited her to a post as Youth Work Field Officer for Victoria and Tasmania. She was lent to the Methodist Church there for three exciting and challenging years just as the Uniting Church was preparing to be born. On her return to Scotland, Dr Horace Walker, Secretary of the Home Board, suggested she meet with the Rev. Dr Archie Mills who was opening up a new field of church work based on his research in group dynamics. Before long she was working with him as 'Assistant Director of Counselling Development and Training for the Church of Scotland'. This pioneering work led Jean and Dr Mills to train to become Certified Transactional Analysts, finding in psychological theory a tool helpful in equipping Christians to '*love your neighbour as you love yourself*'.

The work spread. They trained those who had taken their courses to train others, equipping them as leaders of house groups and as pastoral counsellors. After Dr. Mills moved to other work, Jean was employed by the Board of Education as 'Group Relations Adviser'. As such she also became a visiting lecturer for nurses, prison officers, social workers and to students in St. Colm's College where she offered courses on Transactional Analysis (T.A.) and pastoral care. With Fr Michael Carroll, she led a Sunday evening series on Scottish Television to help church house groups understand group dynamics.

In 1980 Jean married Bill Morrison. Two years later they were permanent foster parents for two teenagers, and Jean left employment to be a full-time mum. Once they were settled as a family, Jean was appointed as the first Director of the Pastoral Foundation in Edinburgh, to set up an ecumenical counselling service. Counselling was still in its infancy in Scotland. Jean saw the need for this work to be accredited by a secular agency as well as being part of the Church's outreach. She became an accredited counsellor with the British Association for Counselling, then later took further training in London to be one of their accredited supervisors. The work grew, and a staff team developed. A three-year part-time course evolved to train voluntary counsellors, with secular accreditation. The Pastoral Foundation then offered a 10 day training course in counselling supervision open to counsellors accredited by other agencies. Jean taught this with two colleagues, supervisors with Couple Counselling backgrounds. Another popular development was a 13 morning training for bereavement care teams – clergy with their selected lay people from various denominations.

All through these developments the Presbytery of Edinburgh had recognized Jean's work as appropriate for the office of Deacon. After eight years Jean decided to go into private practice as a counsellor, supervisor and trainer in the wider community. She was shocked – and hurt – to discover that this move made her ineligible for membership of the courts of the Church, under church law. The Diaconate still accepted her work as that of an Active Deacon, much to her relief.

Jean was invited to join the Steering Group to review Supervision Accreditation within the British Association for Counselling, and became vice-chair of their new Supervision Accreditation

Management Group. She graduated Doctor of Psychotherapy through Professional Studies in the summer of 2003. In retirement she was actively involved in organising retreat days for Deacons.

Jean is the author of a number of training books and booklets, amongst them:[xxvii]

* *Grow to Love - Developing Caring Relationships: a Resource Book for Groups* (1977 & 1980)
* *A Tool for Christians Book 1* (1980 & 1993) and *A Tool for Christians Book 2* (1983) were the first British publications teaching and applying the theory of Transactional Analysis.
* *Growing Fellowship - Six 'Do-It-Yourself' Bible Studies For Woman's Guild Meetings* (1982)
* *What on earth is God like? - Three Bible Studies* (1985)
* *Family Relationships* (1985) / *Challenging Relationships* (1985) / *Marriage Relationships* (1987) / *Work Relationships* (1985) - relational Bible Study booklets commissioned by the British and Foreign Bible Society.
* *Loss - an Invitation to Grow* (1986)
    Her involvement in training counsellors with a disability led to her studying for a doctorate and subsequently writing her last book:
* *Wake up to Your Dreams : An Exploration of Disability and Ability in Dreams* (2005: with John Lowrie Morrison)

Moyra McCallum

Moyra McCallum was commissioned on 17 October 1965 in Woodside South Church, Aberdeen; she went on to do research at St Andrew's University from 1965 to 69 before taking up an appointment as Assistant Lecturer in Biblical Studies, Aberdeen for a year. She served at Northfield Aberdeen from 1970 to 71.

A tutor at St Colm's from 1971 to 94, Moyra taught Biblical Studies, Diaconal Studies and Devotional Studies. She had the gift of bringing the Bible to life in her Old Testament lectures, teaching with such clarity that note-taking was unnecessary and I for one can still hear her voice when I read certain O.T. passages. My own visit to Qumran a few years ago immediately brought her lectures on the

Dead Sea Scrolls back to mind. In Diaconal Studies, as well as the history of the Diaconate, she raised lots of practical issues about living alone which was invaluable for going into a parish. In devotional studies she introduced us to Christian Mystics, the Desert Fathers, and to contemplative writers. Moyra inspired, encouraged and challenged us and, although one of the tutors, was always one of us. She continues to be the confidant of many when needed.

Sheena McNaughton

Sheena McNaughton was appointed by the Home Board to a new area of service in 1969 when she became Field Secretary for Playgroups in the Fife Area. She had previously served as a Parish Deaconess in both Castlemilk and Glenrothes in their early days and on her resignation from the Home Board in 1977 her experience of children and playgroups led to her appointment as Organiser to Fife Regional Council's Services Committee on the Pre-School Child.

When asked by a playgroup colleague if she felt she had 'Leapt over the wall', she said that she was not conscious of any high jumps – only that the work needed to be done and that God had no barriers.

Rhoda Drummond

Rhoda Drummond was commissioned in Hamilton Bardrainey Church, Port Glasgow, before going to work with the Church of Scotland Huts and Canteens Committee in Germany. In 1970 she was asked to become a Chaplain's Assistant in the RAF and served for seventeen years. Her work involved her visiting WRAF girls and young wives and mothers in the RAF quarters, taking services, and Bible studies. Although she wore RAF uniform she had no rank which meant she was an equal with whatever rank she was speaking to. When she retired she was given a flight in a 'Red Arrow'.

Lynda Wright

Lynda was involved in setting up a Columban Community in 1983, consisting of three flats in a stair of six in a Muirhouse tenement. The occupants tried to live as a family, sharing possessions and money, providing a base for hospitality in the neighbourhood. They met daily for prayers in the morning and shared the evening meal together in the home of whoever was doing the cooking for that day. They also committed to spending one evening per week together for Bible Study, discussion on practicalities and worship.

Lynda's next period of Community was at the Abbey Centre, Iona, for three years. Lynda was to fulfil her dream of having a retreat house where people could rediscover themselves and renew their faith when she began the work at Key House (1993-2010), offering a place of prayer and retreat for individuals or where groups could go for guided quiet days. Working in Chaplaincy with NHS Fife she is involved in the pioneering work of developing Community Chaplaincy, going out as Chaplain to the doctors' surgeries.

Yvonne Teague

Yvonne Teague (nee Lynn) was one of the Irish Deaconesses who studied at St Colm's. She was appointed in 1968 by the Home Board to work as Hospital Chaplain. The Deaconess Board agreed to accept her as a Deaconess in the Church of Scotland. In 1988 Yvonne was appointed as fulltime secretary to the Diaconate Committee. In 1992 her post changed to work partly with the Diaconate Committee and partly as Educational Development Officer within the Board of Ministry and later the Ministries Council. This involved her in pre and post ordination courses for the Ministry of Word and Sacrament, Auxiliary and Diaconate Ministries.

Jessie Adamson

Jessie Adamson in retirement received a pension from four Committees of the Church, having worked for a time with each of them. She served with the Overseas Council in India. She was commissioned in 1960 by the Presbytery of Northern Europe in St Martin's Garrison Church in Lemgo having gone to work with The Huts and Canteens Committee. She also served for a time with the National Bible Society of Scotland before being appointed by the Home Board. She had to come home from India because she needed an operation which was predicted to give her only another three years of life: she in fact survived another thirty years.

Irene Glass

Irene Glass worked for 30 years in India in Rajasthan, working amongst the women as Principal of a Girls School and as Hostel Superintendent. In 1956 she was appointed a Church Sister of the United Church of North India. On her return to Scotland she was acknowledged as a Deaconess on the retired list.

Irene in her retirement took it on herself to carry out a very special ministry. As part of the fellowship of the Diaconate we have a Birthday prayer list when we can remember each other in our devotions on the day of the month of the date of our Birthday. Irene began a ministry of phoning the person on their actual Birthday, having a brief chat with them and promising to remember them in her prayers for the next year. Over the years we all came to appreciate Irene's phone call to the extent that after her death it was decided to continue the link by having a small group of four who would share the responsibility of the birthday phone calls.

Mark Evans

Mark Evans, currently the longest serving male Deacon, was commissioned in 1988 – the Centenary year of the Diaconate.

Mark had wanted to be a minister for as long as he could remember. In his childhood games he would play at being a minister while his friends chose football and cowboys and Indians. At the end of fourth year at Ainslie Park School when his class mates were going into local firms or getting jobs as ancillary workers at the Western General hospital, he was told by guidance staff to forget about being a minister and to consider a 'real' job, such as an Occupational Therapist or working for the Forestry Commission. He was one of the few pupils to return to school for a sixth year.

Then at a youth event on ministry, after hearing the text from Isaiah 43: 1 (*'Fear not: for I have redeemed you, I have called you by your name; you are mine'*) he spoke to Ada Younger, the Church of Scotland National Youth Advisor, about wanting to be a minister. Ada arranged to meet with him and to explain the process about selection school, university and divinity degrees. Mark recalls that '*It was as if dreams had been snatched from me in an instant*' – the process was so onerous. Ada, however, arranged for him to join a Summer Mission Team during the school holidays and helped him to apply to St Colm's as an independent student. The original plan was for him to go to St Colm's until he could apply to '121' for selection school.

Mark said: '*It only took a few months for me to realise that Ministry of Word and Sacrament was not for me and during a College Quiet Day I was walking in the Botanic Gardens – wondering on what that passage from Isaiah meant to me. I was going around the Rock Garden when I met Maureen and Ian Hutchison – and it suddenly became clear – I knew with a clarity and a certainty that God was calling me to Diaconal Ministry… to follow in the footsteps of the 'deacs' I knew from growing up in the Old Kirk, Pilton: Maureen, Morag and Lynda'*.

He spoke with Moyra McCallum about returning to St Colm's for a second year to complete the 'Certificate of Diaconal Studies' and to explore the process of applying to become a candidate with Ministry and Mission. The first step was with the Diaconate Committee but the response he received from the Committee was less than enthusiastic. The next step was an interview over tea and scones at the Roxburgh Hotel with Dr Doyle from the Ministry and Mission Committee. Dr Doyle asked '*Why waste your time trying to be a Deacon. You should think about being a Minister – we need young men like you*'. Shortly after this, Mary Levison visited St Colm's and Mark spoke to her of his dream of being a Deacon and his sense of frustration with the Church. She too had experienced frustrations and reminded him of the first part of the Isaiah verse '*Fear not*'!

Mark was accepted as a candidate for the Diaconate and as he wasn't a candidate from Ministry and Mission he had to find a post where he could serve his probationary year.

A job with the Board of Social Responsibility at the People's Palace was offered and Mark was able to complete his probationary period there. Next, discussion took place between the Diaconate Committee and Edinburgh Presbytery in relation to his commissioning. Although the Diaconate had been opened to men since 1979 no one man had come forward (though there were plans for the Lay Missionaries to join the Diaconate en-masse). It had been hoped that as the first male candidate Mark's commissioning would be part of the Centenary Celebrations ... but then some one noticed his date of birth and pointed out he was too young and couldn't be commissioned till October – after his 21st birthday!! Mark Evans was commissioned in the Old Kirk of Edinburgh that October by the Moderator of Edinburgh Presbytery, the Rev. Mary Levison, and he had Maureen Hutchison DCS as one of his sponsors. The Presbytery of Lothian meanwhile had commissioned Graham Austin as the first trained male Deacon in the Church of Scotland on 8 September 1988 – although the Lay Missionaries had all been commissioned at a special service in June.

Work at the People's Palace saw Mark working with young men and boys involved in the 'sex industry'. It was the late 80's and the shadow of HIV / AIDs was a real threat – and the predictions of the numbers infected (and affected) were terrifying. It was an interest he wanted to develop – so after discussions with colleagues and Social Responsibility he applied to the North Lothian College of Nursing & Midwifery to train as a nurse. This signalled a new battle with the Church. He had only just become a Deacon but was put on the 'supplementary list' for despite the Diaconate's own heritage he couldn't remain on the active list whilst undertaking nurse training.

On applying to National Mission in 1994 to become a 'Parish Assistant', Mark had to go back to St Colm's for 'formation' training for a year. In 1995 he was appointed to Christ's Kirk, Glenrothes, as Parish Assistant leading the congregation's pastoral ministry and work with children and young people. While there, in 1998, he was invited to participate in discussions about piloting a new ministry, Interim Ministry, helping congregations to rediscover their calling and vision. In June 1998 he was offered a secondment as an 'Interim Deacon' within the Board of Ministry and was sent to work in the joint congregations of the Breich Valley.

At the end of Mark's time there he was offered a post by Colinton Parish Church as Parish Deacon leading the congregation's Children & Youth Ministry. During this time he continued study using his experience of Pastoral Ministry to graduate from University with a degree in Health Studies.

As a result of his studies Mark applied for the post of Hospital Chaplain with NHS Fife and started in the Queen Margaret Hospital Dunfermline in March 2006. In 2011 he was appointed Head of Spiritual Care for NHS Fife, responsible for strategic development and service delivery, managing a team of Healthcare Chaplains, denominational chaplains and pastoral volunteers. Contemporary hospital chaplaincy seeks a balanced approach that is flexible and responsive to the diverse spiritual and pastoral needs of modern society.

In 2010 Mark had started post-graduate studies in Healthcare Chaplaincy at Glasgow University from which he graduated with a MSc in November 2012. Following these studies, he was offered a secondment with NHS Education for Scotland as National Project Lead (Spiritual Care) – working with the Belief Communities to develop spiritual care within health and social care settings. He is a member of the Scottish Government's 'Death Certification Advisory Group', of NHS Scotland's 'Death Certification Programme Group' and also of the National Coordinating Group for the Scottish Grief and Bereavement Hub. Within the Church of Scotland he serves on the Presbytery of Edinburgh's Strategy Group and on a Focus Group established to explore future development of The Guild.

In Healthcare Chaplaincy Mark found a ministry that combined the love of nursing and health care with his call to a ministry of service.

Lewis Rose

After Lewis Rose had spent over thirty yeas of his working life at sea, he wanted to give something of himself to society. He applied to National Mission and was accepted to train at St Colm's towards the end of 1980s. The residential training brought him and others into living and working with people whom they would otherwise have had no contact with. He appreciated the diverse group of people, from different cultures and backgrounds, enabling differing social, theological and political views to be heard and expressed. For him the training gave a breadth of experience and he appreciated the experienced supervisors he had in his placements which were with the chaplaincy team at the Royal Edinburgh Hospital and a Social Responsibility project as well as two parish attachments which had different theological perspectives. His summer project was spent working with Scottish Churches Industrial Mission.

He was appointed to Camperdown Parish Church, Dundee. There he became involved with the Community Business Dundee and Dundee West Victim Support where he became chairperson. He was on the steering committee for setting up the Credit Union, enabling a local person to become chair. He became involved with Church Action on Poverty taking a group of people to London to tell their story. He was also involved in setting up a youth project for 11 to 15 year olds. This involved securing funding and the appointment of a youth worker and volunteers to help run the project.

After six years it was time to move on from Dundee. Scottish Churches Industrial Mission were looking to appoint an Organiser for the North of Scotland based in Aberdeen: Lewis applied and was successful. One of the most important aspects for Industrial Mission is building up relationships both within the churches and outside of them.

One of the first things that Lewis did when he moved to Aberdeen and the North of Scotland was to learn and understand the culture.

He visited firms and organisations hearing about their work and the contribution they made to the economy and society locally, nationally and internationally. He was also involved in relationships at a strategic level: the STUC, Chambers of Commerce, individual trade unions, Local Councils, and the Scottish Parliament. Today industry is concerned about targets, deadlines and profits; and employees are seen as a resource for companies and shareholders to achieve these things. Lewis believes that it is therefore of prime importance that Workplace Chaplaincy as it is now called 'loiters with intent' in the workplace and is seen as relevant by both industry and commerce and most importantly the Church, looking at issues from a theological stance.

13

World DIAKONIA and Ecumenical Connections

*'I sent them into the world, just as you sent me into the world.... I
pray that they may all be one.'*
(John 17: 18, 21a)

*'Christian love is absurd and unreasonable, because it is a love over
and above all boundaries."* (Pastor Edwall, Swedish President of
DIAKONIA: St Giles Cathedral, 13 July 1966)

World DIAKONIA is the world federation of Sisterhoods and
Diaconal Associations which brings together ecumenically Deacons,
Deaconesses and Diaconal workers from many different traditions
and different countries. DIAKONIA was born out of a longing for
reconciliation and healing in the aftermath of World War II. Many
Motherhouses in Europe were in ruin and the question for them was
how to make a new start. It was the federation of Deaconess Houses
in the Netherlands who took steps to contact their colleagues in
Switzerland, France, Scandinavia and North America after the war.
When the first Conference was planned Germany was not present as
it would have been difficult for the Dutch Deaconesses who had
suffered much in the war. However Germany was able to be included
at the next Conference.

DIAKONIA was founded at the conference in Copenhagen in 1947.
As DIAKONIA grew it was split into three regions: DIAKONIA of
the Americas and Caribbean (DOTAC); DIAKONIA Region Africa
Europe (DRAE); and DIAKONIA Asia Pacific (DAP). World
DIAKONIA Assemblies are held every four years with the Regional
Assemblies in the intervening years.

The Church of Scotland has been well represented on the Executive
of DIAKONIA over the years since the beginning when we were
represented by Margaret Allan DCS, Rina Grainger DCS, Mary

Levison (Lusk) DCS and Kay Ramsay DCS who was editor of the English Edition of *DIAKONIA News* for a time and also editor of the book *DIAKONIA Challenge and Response.*[xxviii]

Scotland was host country to the DIAKONIA Assembly in 1966 bringing together 250 participants from five Continents and nineteen countries. The President of our Deaconess Council, Dorothy Gardner, had invited them to come to Scotland at the close of the conference in Berlin in 1963. The theme of the week-long conference was 'New paths for Diakonia'. It included speakers, Bible exposition led by Professor Robert Davidson, and a Civic Reception hosted by the Lord Provost of Edinburgh. There were opportunities to meet in small groups; a Garden Party was held at Carberry; and a tour included visiting the new town of Glenrothes as well as seeing the beauty spots of Callander and the Trossachs.

In 1994 Scotland hosted the first DIAKONIA Region Africa Europe Conference at Stirling University. Previously there had been a European Region but this conference was to agree a constitution which would include Africa in the Region. The 260 delegates came from fourteen European and six African countries. It was said before the Conference that it would be important to have at least one African at the conference, so the Deacons in Scotland set themselves the task to raise funds to bring at least one African. In the event they sponsored four Africans, three Hungarians and two Icelanders as well as subsidising costs for Deacons from Scotland and the rest of the UK. The theme of the conference 'Behold I make all things new' was woven into every aspect of it from the Bible study led by Moyra McCallum DCS and the speakers from Hungary, Zambia, Scotland and Sweden who spoke of the new challenges for Diaconal service. The daily sessions were led by music from the Scottish Deacons. The highlight of the conference was the session, 'Exploring sources of Church Music' led by Rev. John Bell. One elderly German Deaconess was heard to say *'The music was so beautiful I thought I was in heaven'*. Still today many Deaconesses speak fondly of their time in Scotland. Congregations where Deacons worked hosted groups at worship on the Sunday. Speakers from the Conference went to other congregations who did not have a Deacon and to churches who had been supportive in raising funds to bring delegates from Africa. Hospitality after these services provided opportunities for congregations to learn more of Diaconal work world-wide. The Woman's Guild through the Presbyterial Councils had provided postcards, tea-towels and sweets for the welcome bags as well as hospitality at the tea stops for the six coaches on the tours to Callander, Crieff or the Trossachs. Two coaches (90 people) headed north after the Conference to tour the Highlands and visit the islands of Skye and Iona. Once again hospitality was provided by the Guilds. Much work went into the planning but so many of the lovely stories we heard afterwards – of unexpected coincidences of people meeting up with people – were not of our doing but the work of a greater hand than ours.

For the Deacons it was an important way of raising the profile of the Diaconate because just weeks before the conference we had received two major blows. The first when National Mission for financial reasons decided to end residential training at St Colm's and the second was the news that those in training would not have salaried places in 1994-95. This second decision was overthrown by the Assembly and the salaries were found.

Jane Martin DCS while undertaking her work as a parish Deaconess in Chalmers Ardler Church in Dundee was the Church of Scotland's representative on the United Kingdom Liaison Group for DIAKONIA; being asked to serve as Secretary to that group, she therefore became the UK representative on the Executive Committee of World DIAKONIA in 1987. She was elected as Vice President of DIAKONIA Region Africa Europe at Stirling in 1994 and two years later, at the DIAKONIA World Assembly in Friedrichroda, Germany, was to be elected President. During her time as President she visited the Motherhouses in Hungary and made a particular point of visiting the African Associations. She was later to be the English editor of *DIAKONIA News* and was President of the Diaconate Council in Scotland from 1994-97.

SEED ('The Scottish Ecumenical Encounter on the Diaconate') was part of the Centenary Celebrations in 1988. It brought together those involved in or responsible for Diaconal work from the Scottish Episcopal Church, the Methodist Church, the Church of England and the Roman Catholic Church as well as the Church of Scotland and the Presbyterian Church in Ireland. It happened at a time when there was a lot of discussion going on in the different denominations about the place of Diaconal ministry in the Church. The ecumenical dialogue was found to be so worthwhile that it was followed by SEED II in 1991 led by Scottish Episcopal Church and SEED III in 1994 organised by the Roman Catholic Church. It was also to be a springboard for a series of discussions held amongst Deacons throughout the UK which culminated in a conference at St George's, Windsor, where the Windsor Statement was produced and sent to Churches Together in Britain and Ireland for a study by all the denominations into Diaconal ministry. Sadly when it went out to the Churches it died a death. Describing the call to Diaconal ministry, the Statement said:[xxix]

> *'Deacons are continually aware of God's call for the Church to be Christ the Servant in the world and to focus the servant ministry of the whole Church. Deacons in enabling the Diaconal ministry of the Church often hold this task in creative tension with the difficulty the churches have in living out the servant role. The ministry of a Deacon constantly demands vision, direction, breadth and growth; it is radical in outlook and outreach, pioneering in vision. Therefore Deacons develop a rich spirituality to share with the church and the world. ... Deacons have no special powers or activities exclusively reserved to them. What is, however, distinctive is their call to be publicly accountable servants of the church who have charge to model, encourage, and coordinate diakonia. This is the particular call or vocation of the Deacon that is not shared by all Christians.'*

The Diaconate in Scotland has always been small but it has always been at the forefront on the world scene – as it has been in the forefront of mission in Scotland. In all the different traditions the

Diaconate struggles for identity in the Church structures. When budgets are cut the Diaconate is first to go, yet through it all a ministry of service is carried out to those at the margins of society. We are strengthened when we meet with others in fellowship from around the world, coming from different traditions doing different work but all seeking to meet the needs where we are. Sister Uta Hampel, President of DRAE in 1994, summed it up in the opening words of a letter to members of DRAE after the conference in Scotland:

> 'Hope is the ability to hear the music of tomorrow
> and faith is the courage to dance to it today.'

14

Conclusion

'Go into all the world ... and lo I am with you always.'
(Matthew 28:19, 20)

A Story to Tell has traced the journey of the Diaconate in Scotland over 125 years from the early vision of Dr Charteris to where it is today. It has been a ministry thwarted by institutional structures and by a lack of financial resources which have prevented the vision realising its full potential in the earlier years. Charteris' vision was for an office of ministry in the Church, accountable to and ordained by the Church. Today the Diaconate, which began as a women's ministry, has moved on by leaps and bounds in the last twenty years to realise that first vision, but now, as a Diaconate of men and women, taking its place in the courts and structures of the Church and being accountable to the Church – and not merely to an employing body.

Numbers have remained small; but from our Diaconate's earliest days, beginning with single women of independent means, there has been vision and a pioneering spirit as dedicated and determined Deacons have been involved in mission very often at the margins of society, drawing alongside, touching and influencing many lives along the way.

The training from the beginning, at Deaconess House and the St Ninian's Training Institute, was about personal formation and developing the spiritual life, rather than training for a function or task; it held together practice and theory. From the beginning training has developed and changed according to need, setting up the Deaconess Hospital to provide the practical training required for district visiting at that period in time. Over the years the training has continued to adapt and change as both needs in society and/or the needs of employing committees changed, for a period including a specialised training at the end of the formation and theological training. Because of the smallness of numbers we have perhaps lost something of the Diaconal and formational element in the training currently offered, but still those coming forward have a vision to serve the Church and the world through collaborative working.

Few of the Deacons who trained at St Colm's now remain in active service. Many of us valued the residential element and fellowship we experienced in our training and formation. Today Diaconal students train alongside Ministers of Word and Sacrament, perhaps introducing a new element into collegiate ministry. At the time this book was being written, a group was once again looking at training and how it will meet the needs of the Church in the future.

We take heart because our story and struggle is not particular to the Diaconate in Scotland but is reflected around the world in different denominations and different traditions. This has not been a theological study into Diaconal ministry but mainly a local history. Countless books have been written that look at the theology about Diaconal ministry: and similar debates go on around the world.

What is a Deacon?

At one point in time the ministry of the Deacon was described as being the' eyes and ears' of the bishop. Today the Deacon still identifies needs and challenges the church to look at ministry at the margins.
In the Church of Scotland:[xxx] '*A Deacon is a man or woman who, under a Call from God, has pledged himself or herself to the service of Jesus Christ and His Church and has been selected, trained and ordained to exercise a ministry ......according to the doctrine and discipline of the Church of Scotland. The Office of Deacon is*

recognised by the Church to be a distinctive, lifelong status within the ministry of the Church and to be agreeable to the Word of God'.

The charge given to a Deacon on their ordination says:[xxxi] '*In your ministry as a Deacon as well as exercising pastoral care both within and beyond the church, be ready to be a pioneer, revealing needs not fully acknowledged, bringing to light injustices easy to overlook, pointing to tasks most avoid'.*

So what is a Deacon? What do they do? From the stories told in this book it can be seen that no two Deacons do the same thing. The ministry of the Deacon today builds bridges between the Church and a world whose needs are constantly changing; Deacons and the Diaconate are constantly adapting to meet those needs. One invariable is the ability of the Deacon to draw alongside others, enabling them to fulfil their own Diaconal calling in the world.

The ministry of the Deacon has been described as most resembling the ministry of Christ responding to needs.

We do not know what the future holds we can only echo one of the early Church Sisters at the death of Alice Maxwell '*We, her sister Deaconesses, feel that the first chapter in the history of the Diaconate of the Church of Scotland is finished. It remains for us to write a second that will be worthy of its noble beginning'.* As we celebrate our 125th Anniversary another chapter is finished; it remains for us to see that we too, through our ministry as Deacons in the Church, write a new chapter worthy of our noble beginnings and of all those who have gone before us in the service of Christ.

Endnotes

[i] TLS: 'Training in Learning and Service' (or, as later, 'Training in Learning for Serving'): a church-based voluntary study course structured via local groups.

[ii] J. Steele & A. Campbell, *The Story of the Church* (1962) p217.

[iii] A. H. Charteris, *The Church of Christ - The Baird Lecture 1887*, p144.

[iv] Charteris, *op cit.,* p158.

[v] Charteris, *op. cit.,* p163

[vi] *Reports to the General Assembly of the Church of Scotland* (1886) p416.

[vii] *Reports to the General Assembly of the Church of Scotland* (1886) p420.

[viii] M. Magnusson, *Out of Silence: The Woman's Guild 1887-1987* (1987).

[ix] *Reports to the General Assembly of the Church of Scotland* (1887) p425.

[x] A. Gordon, *The Life of Archibald Hamilton Charteris* (c.1912) p356.

[xi] H. Macrae, *Alice Maxwell Deaconess* (1920), p88.

[xii] *Ibid.*

[xiii] F. D. Bardgett, *Devoted Service Rendered - The Lay Missionaries of the Church of Scotland* (2002).

[xiv] *Reports to the General Assembly of the Church of Scotland* (1894) p252.

[xv] M. Levison, *Wrestling with the Church* (1992), p35.

[xvi] D. P. Thomson, *Women of the Scottish Church* (1975), p314.

[xvii] *Diaconate News*, Autumn 2009.

[xviii] *Reports to the General Assembly of the Church of Scotland* (1956), p794.

[xix] *Deaconess Newsletter,* summer 1976.

[xx] *Reports to the General Assembly of the Church of Scotland* (1987), p271.

[xxi] *Reports to the General Assembly of the Church of Scotland* (1989), p204.

[xxii] *The Windsor Statement on the Diaconate* (1997) p4.

xxiii J. Adamson, K. Ramsay & M. Craig, *Stella: The story of Stella Jane Reekie, 1922-1982* (1984).

xxiv *Deaconess Newsletter*, October 1982.

xxv See note 1, above.

xxvi K. Ramsay & the Diakonia Foundation (ed.), *Diakonia: Challenge and Response* (1996). The book contains the following articles: 'Foreword' (Chita R. Framo); 'Africa, Europe and the World' (Kay Ramsay); 'Challenge for the nineties' (Betsy K. Ewing); 'Sacrament of Care' (Inga Bengtzon); 'Companioning Diakonia' (Reinhard Neubauer); 'Diakonia in the Americas and the Caribbean' (Louise Williams); 'Diakonia in the Asia-Pacific Region' (Marjorie McGregor); 'Diakonia in Africa' (Kay Ramsay); 'Into the Future' (Alison McRae).

xxvii If attempting to find these works in catalogues, search under both Jean C. Morrison and Jean C. Grigor.

xxviii See note 26, above.

xxix *The Windsor Statement on the Diaconate* (1997) p23.

xxx The General Assembly of the Church of Scotland: Act VIII (2010) Consolidating and Amending Act Anent Deacons (incorporating the provisions of Acts VIII 1998, IX 2001, VII 2002 and II 2004, all as amended): section 1.

xxxi 'The Church of Scotland Ordinal and Service Book' as cited (November 2013) at website: http://www.churchofscotland.org.uk/serve/the_diaconate